A LOOK BACK AT THE RICH HISTORY
OF THE WWE CHAMPIONSHIP

CHAMPIONSHIP

KEVIN SULLIVAN

World
Wrestling
Entertainment®
BOOKS

SIMON &
SCHUSTER

This book is a publication of Simon & Schuster UK Ltd under exclusive license
from World Wrestling Entertainment, Inc.

This Simon & Schuster paperback edition November 2011

Designed by Ruth Lee-Mui

Printed and bound by CPI Group (UK) Ltd, Croydon, CR0 4YY

10 9 8 7 6 5 4 3 2 1

ISBN 978-0-85720-687-9

INTRODUCTION

Each year, thousands of young men step into wrestling rings around the world with hopes of one day reaching the top of the sports-entertainment mountain. But only the absolute elite earn entry into the global phenomenon of WWE; and of these select few, only a fraction possess the drive, determination, and innate skill required to capture the industry's richest prize: the WWE Championship.

Over the course of its nearly fifty-year history, WWE and its flagship title have gone through several name changes. In its earliest days, the company was known as the Capitol Wrestling Corporation, a small promotion governed by wrestling powerhouse the National Wrestling Alliance. Capitol Wrestling broke away from the NWA in 1963 to form its own stand-alone company called World Wide Wrestling Federation. In 1979 the name was shortened to World Wrestling Federation. And finally in 2002, the company adopted its current name, World Wrestling Entertainment. For the sake of consistency, this book will mainly reference both the company and the championship under their current labels (WWE and WWE Championship), regardless of the time period.

In the pages that follow, the story of the WWE Championship will be told like never before. Along the way, you'll relive the events that helped elevate the title to its lofty status, as well as learn the true stories that unfolded behind the scenes. The Iron Sheik's refusal to be bought off by the rival AWA. Sgt. Slaughter's threats on his life. Ric Flair's internal struggles before finally jumping to WWE. Steve Austin's meteoric rise to superstardom. John Cena's battle for respect. Every champion's true story gets told here.

The WWE Championship has no equal. It represents the absolute pinnacle of the wrestling world. And for its holders, it means instant access into the most elite fraternity in all of sports-entertainment.

Less than fifty men have successfully etched their names into the record books. And this is their story. It's time to grab your front-row seat and be guided through the long and storied history of the WWE Championship.

1

NORTHEAST SUPREMACY

There are only a handful of matches that sports-entertainment historians regularly point to as the most pivotal performances in WWE Championship history: Bruno Sammartino's quick defeat of Buddy Rogers in May 1963; Hulk Hogan's drubbing of the Iron Sheik in January 1984; Shawn Michaels's highly controversial victory over Bret Hart in the now-infamous November 1997 Montreal Screwjob. But amazingly, the most influential title match in WWE history may have actually taken place before the company ever existed.

On June 30, 1961, nearly two years before WWE sold its first ticket, Buddy Rogers challenged Pat O'Connor for the National Wrestling Alliance World Heavyweight Championship at Chicago's Comiskey Park. In front of more than 38,000 fans, the cocky Rogers claimed the prestigious title that fateful night, thus ending O'Connor's remarkable two-and-a-half-year reign. While winning the gold was certainly impressive, on the surface the victory simply appeared to be your run-of-the-mill title change. But in reality, Rogers's NWA Championship win actually helped set the wheels in motion for the creation of the global phenomenon known today as WWE.

To fully comprehend how Buddy Rogers's victory eventually resulted in the formation of WWE, it is important to understand how the Northeast wrestling territory was operated during this time and, most important, Vincent J. McMahon's rise to power within the region and his subsequent use of Rogers.

Vincent J., the father of current WWE chairman Vincent K. McMahon, grew up in and around the businesses of boxing and wrestling. As the son of popular promoter Jess McMahon, he was afforded a firsthand education that other promoters could only dream of obtaining. This behind-the-scenes access into the wrestling world's inner workings helped catapult Vincent J. into a very prominent position at a relatively young age. At just twenty years old, he began promoting his own fights out of Hempstead, New York, in 1935. But before he could make a serious name for himself within the Northeast territory, the up-and-coming promoter was shipped to North Carolina to serve in the United States Coast Guard during World War II. The move set McMahon's professional career back several years, but he refused to let it permanently derail his dreams.

When the time came for McMahon to get back into the business, the New York territory was already under the control of successful promoter Joseph "Toots" Mondt. This forced McMahon to take his passion for the squared circle elsewhere. He eventually landed in Washington, D.C., where he began managing Turner's Arena, a dilapidated old building once owned by former middleweight wrestling champion William "Joe" Turner. Over the next four years, McMahon promoted concerts and weekly wrestling events out of Turner's Arena before eventually buying the facility outright in December 1952.

Now with an established arena as part of his portfolio, McMahon

Pat O'Connor (left).

went right to work creating his own wrestling company; and on January 7, 1953, he put on his first show under the Capitol Wrestling Corporation banner. Like most startups, Capitol Wrestling experienced its fair share of uncertainty in the beginning. But the company's fortunes eventually solidified when McMahon embraced the power of television, a new media that many promoters didn't necessarily understand at the time.

On January 5, 1956, McMahon aired the first-ever Capitol Wrestling television program. The show was an instant hit, and within six months Capitol Wrestling was in high demand as far north as the coveted New York market. This was the opening McMahon needed: With Joe Mondt— New York's chief promoter—temporarily sidelined, he was able to promote his product at famed Madison Square Garden.

Capitol Wrestling proved very popular with the MSG fans, which infuriated Mondt. But once the public got a taste of McMahon's company, there was very little anybody could do to stop the momentum coming from the nation's capital, and by 1960 McMahon had emerged as the clear victor of the battle for the Northeast.

Following the fight for Northeast supremacy, McMahon shocked the wrestling world when he welcomed former adversary Toots Mondt into Capitol Wrestling as a partner. Together, the duo accomplished countless successes, but none were as important as the acquisition of Buddy Rogers.

At the time, the original "Nature Boy" was regarded as one of the greatest wrestlers in the world, complete with more than forty championship reigns from promotions all over North America. He was also one of the most hated, largely due to the arrogant aura he emitted while competing in the ring. But despite his less-than-favorable personality, Rogers had a knack for drawing sellout crowds wherever he went. And once McMahon and Mondt assumed his booking rights, those sellout crowds became their sellout crowds, as the duo booked the majority of his matches to take place in their Northeast territory.

In June 1961, Capitol Wrestling joined forces with Chicago's Fred Kohler to promote the historic encounter that saw Rogers end Pat O'Connor's epic reign as NWA Champion. NWA promoters nationwide saw Rogers's win as a golden opportunity to bring wrestling's biggest draw to their territories, as it was commonplace during this period for the NWA Champion to travel from promotion to promotion defending the title.

But McMahon and Mondt saw things differently. Utilizing their booking power over Rogers, they scheduled nearly all of the champ's matches to take place in their territory. In fact, from March 1961 to May 1963, Rogers main-evented twenty-three of the twenty-six MSG events put on by Capitol Wrestling. As a result of this unusually protective style of booking, legendary names such as Stu Hart, Jim Crockett, and Don Owen were deprived of the chance to promote championship matches in their territories. Unfortunately for them, there was very little they could do to better their situation. Instead, they were practically forced to stand idly by as Capitol Wrestling got rich off of Rogers's NWA Championship reign.

Having had enough, the other promoters within the NWA eventually decided that Rogers defending the title almost exclusively in the Northeast was no longer acceptable. They banded together in the search for an adversary lofty enough to unseat the Nature Boy. In the end, they reached out to the great Lou Thesz, who agreed to come out of retirement for another opportunity at the title he had proudly held four times prior. Much to the joy of every wrestling promoter outside of the Northeast, Thesz was able to dethrone Rogers in Toronto on January 14, 1963. By this time, though, Buddy Rogers and Capitol Wrestling had outgrown the NWA. During Rogers's nineteen months as the titlist, Capitol Wrestling used its unique stranglehold on the NWA title to help solidify itself as the preeminent wrestling company in the nation, regularly sell out MSG, and produce the most popular wrestling product on television. The title was no longer theirs, but the attention of the ticket-purchasing public certainly was.

Buddy Rogers,
the first-ever
champion.

2

THE BREAKAWAY

While NWA promoters celebrated Buddy Rogers's loss, Vincent

J. McMahon and Toots Mondt were busy planning their next

move. Their first course of action was to protest the way in

which the Nature Boy lost the title. At the time, it was common-

place for all championship matches to be contested under

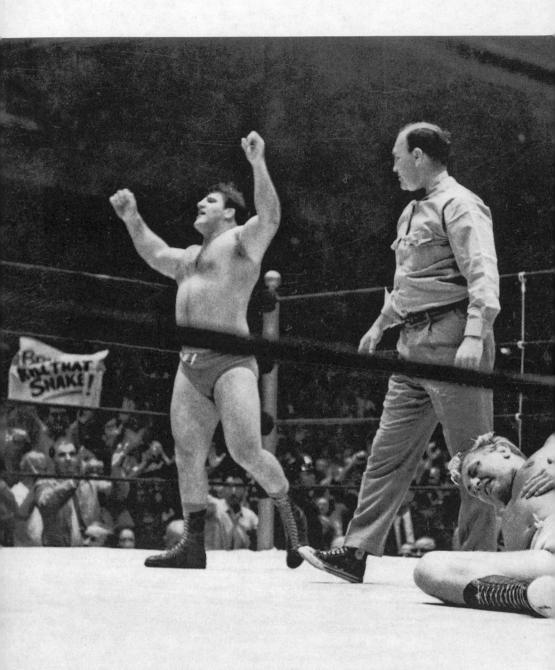

Bruno Sammartino defeats Buddy Rogers.

two-out-of-three falls rules. Rogers's loss, however, occurred in a single-fall contest.

The protest caused what appeared to be a certain degree of conflict between Capitol Wrestling and the NWA. In reality, though, McMahon and Mondt were simply using the controversy as the excuse they needed to finally break away from the NWA. In the end, after a well-orchestrated argument over the validity of Rogers's loss, McMahon and Mondt chose not to recognize the title change. Instead, they withdrew Capitol Wrestling from the NWA as planned and formed their own promotion, which they called World Wide Wrestling Federation.

In April 1963, McMahon and Mondt launched the new brand with their hand-picked Superstar, Buddy Rogers, leading the charge as champion. It didn't take much for fans to buy into the new promotion. They loved to hate the flamboyant Rogers and fully expected to spend the next several years vociferously jeering him.

But shortly before the new promotion officially kicked off, Rogers's career and life nearly came to an end when a heart attack stopped the Superstar in his tracks. The incident, coupled with nearly a quarter-century worth of ring action, was beginning to take its toll on the forty-two-year-old champion. But as long as the gold was around his waist, the Nature Boy was going to fight, and his first true challenge came in the form of twenty-seven-year-old Bruno Sammartino.

The two Superstars met on May 17, 1963, inside the hallowed Madison Square Garden. After just forty-eight seconds of action, Sammartino used his Italian backbreaker to force Rogers into submission, thus ending the first-ever WWE Championship reign.

Nearly fifty years later, despite its brevity, Rogers's time with the gold is looked upon with great fondness. The credibility his powerful name and résumé helped bring to the young title, coupled with his fearless trail-blazing efforts, are major reasons why today's champions are held in such high esteem.

3

SEVEN YEARS, EIGHT MONTHS, ONE DAY

Despite Bruno Sammartino's age and strength advantage, many fans were shocked to see the newcomer manhandle such a legendary competitor as Buddy Rogers. But to those who knew Sammartino intimately, the victory was a mere formality. The Bruno Sammartino they knew was a fighter who

Bruno Sammartino.

had spent much of his life overcoming insurmountable odds just to survive. After watching him stare death in the eye without even blinking, they knew there was no limit to what Sammartino could accomplish.

As a young boy, Bruno and his family spent fourteen months hiding from the Nazis in the mountains of Abruzzo, Italy. During that time, rheumatic fever nearly claimed the future WWE Champion. But he refused to give up, and when World War II finally ended, the Sammartinos traveled to Pittsburgh with hopes of starting anew.

For fourteen-year-old Bruno, life was considerably easier than what he was forced to endure in the mountains. However, he wasn't exactly living the American dream; his schoolmates regularly tormented him for his inability to properly speak English. At just eighty pounds, the foreign newcomer could do little to stop the physical harassment of the larger bullies.

One day, after being pushed around one too many times, a determined Sammartino walked into his local YMCA. He began an extensive weight-lifting program, and within two years he had bulked up to an impressive

Ivan Koloff vs. Bruno Sammartino.

257 pounds. Needless to say, the bullying ceased, but Sammartino's growing passion for weightlifting did not. By the end of 1959, he had owned world records for the bench press (569 pounds), squat (715 pounds), and deadlift (700 pounds).

A professional wrestling career was the logical next step for the accomplished weightlifter. Sammartino made his pro debut in 1959, defeating Dmitri Grabowski in a mere nineteen seconds. The large Italian fan base in New York became instantly enamored by their hulking countryman, and within six months he was headlining Madison Square Garden. But his career hit an unexpected speed bump after being suspended by many states' athletic commissions for unknowingly missing a match due to a scheduling snafu. As a result, finding work in the United States became a difficult task, so he took his game north of the border. The move proved seamless for Sammartino, who was welcomed with open arms by Toronto's large Italian population.

After learning that Sammartino's popularity transcended borders, McMahon and Mondt quickly paid his state athletic commission fines and lured him back to Capitol Wrestling fulltime in February 1963. Three months later, he defeated Buddy Rogers to become history's second-ever WWE Champion. For Sammartino, the win kicked off a meteoric rise in popularity that reached well beyond the ring. Even the pope was a fan: After learning of Sammartino's exploits, Pope Paul VI happily welcomed the champ to the Vatican for a private visit.

Alongside manager Arnold Skaaland, Sammartino tirelessly toured the globe, helping to give the newly formed championship its prestigious *world* title recognition. But it was in New York's Madison Square Garden where the champ had his greatest successes against the likes of Gorilla Monsoon, Hans Mortier, Gene Kiniski, Dr. Jerry Graham, and Killer Kowalski, who was generally regarded as the biggest threat to Sammartino during the 1960s. The two Superstars battled in some of history's most brutal matches, most notably a vicious Stretcher Match under the stars at Boston's famed Fenway Park. The champ successfully retained the title that night after nailing Kowalski with a wooden chair.

By 1971, Sammartino's nearly eight years with the gold saw him turn back all comers, large and small, leaving many spectators to assume he would simply never lose. But with the Cold War at its height, those fans saw their worst fears realized when the Russian Ivan Koloff stunned a sold-out MSG crowd, pinning Sammartino in the middle of the ring following a kneedrop from the top rope.

Bruno Sammartino didn't have the charisma of The Rock, nor did he possess the technical prowess of Bret Hart. But he had the power of an ox and the uncanny ability to draw the fans' support. For an unprecedented seven years, eight months, and one day, those fans stood behind their champion as he reached heights never before seen. But on January 18, 1971, it all came crashing down when the WWE Championship fell into the possession of the dreaded Russian Bear.

Pedro Morales, the fourth
WWE champion.

4

A REASON TO CHEER

As Ivan Koloff was pinning Bruno Sammartino's shoulders to the mat, a young Superstar was back in the Madison Square Garden locker room packing his bag after a successful debut. With just one WWE match on his résumé, not many Northeast fans knew much about the newcomer. But in three weeks time, the entire nation would soon be celebrating Pedro Morales.

Originally from the small Puerto Rican island of Culebra, Morales moved to Brooklyn to live with his aunt when he was just a boy. Like most young Latinos in his borough, he grew up idolizing Miguel Perez, a mainstay on the MSG wrestling scene. Once he became old enough, Morales decided to follow in his hero's footsteps and become a professional wrestler.

Still a teenager at the time, Morales bounced around New York's smaller venues for several years. It wasn't until January 1963 that he received his big break, teaming with his idol Miguel Perez to battle the Tolos Brothers at Madison Square Garden. His brief time in the spotlight caught the eye of legendary West Coast competitor Fred Blassie, who urged Morales to take his game to Los Angeles.

While wrestling in the City of Angels, Morales really started to hone his technical skills, as well as develop that fiery temper he would later become famous for. He went on to capture the territory's heavyweight championship on two occasions, defeating The Destroyer and Luke Graham. This valuable time at the top of the card offered Morales his first taste of the main event, an experience he would later draw from to gain WWE success.

With a wealth of wrestling knowledge now under his belt, Morales returned to New York on January 18, 1971—the same night Ivan Koloff ended Bruno Sammartino's historic reign. The Russian Bear's shocking victory kicked off the most terrifying title reign WWE fans had ever seen. Luckily for them, though, their fears would soon subside.

A mere three weeks after capturing the WWE Championship, Ivan Koloff put his gold on the line against newcomer Pedro Morales at MSG. A late-match belly-to-back suplex by the champ appeared to give Koloff the win, but he failed to take his own shoulders off the mat while the referee made the three count. Morales, on the other hand, did manage to get a shoulder up at the last second. For a brief moment, a sense of confusion fell over the audience; everyone had not witnessed Morales lift his shoulder late in the count. But when the referee finally walked over to Morales and raised his hand in victory, the crowd erupted. Even Bruno Sammartino joined in the celebration. Unable to contain his emotions, the former champ bolted from the locker room to congratulate the fourth Superstar to ever hold the WWE Championship.

After toppling the hated Russian, Pedro Morales became an instant hero to fans everywhere, especially the large Puerto Rican population in

Pedro Morales vs. Ivan Koloff.

New York. At the time, a good portion of the area's immigrants were living in poverty. To them, Morales as WWE Champion provided a reason to cheer, a chance to temporarily leave their worries behind.

"Ethnicity played a big role in Pedro's success," recalls WWE Hall of Famer Howard Finkel. "He was a god. I was a fan back then and I would attend a lot of shows; there were always a large number of Puerto Rican fans there. They believed in him. That is one of those things that is so pertinent."

Behind the support of his fellow Latinos, Pedro Morales proudly defended the WWE Championship for nearly three years. Only Bruno Sammartino, Hulk Hogan, and Bob Backlund have held the title longer. Over the course of his epic reign, Morales successfully turned back such future Hall of Famers as George "The Animal" Steele, Baron Mikel Scicluna, and Ernie Ladd. He even battled fellow fan favorite Bruno Sammartino to a seventy-five-minute time-limit draw at New York's Shea Stadium.

Like Sammartino, it appeared Morales would hold the gold forever, which is why the events of December 1, 1973, were so unexpected.

Morales agreed to put the WWE Championship on the line in Philadelphia against Stan "The Man" Stasiak, a Superstar who gained much of his notoriety competing in the Pacific Northwest and Canada. He had already had a few brief runs with WWE but nothing that stood out as exceptional. On this night, though, The Man would forever etch his name in the annals of sports-entertainment history when he pinned Morales to claim the championship. News of Stasiak's win swept like wildfire across the nation, and fans everywhere began to loathe the man who had knocked off their champion. At home, however, the new champ was a bit of a hero.

"I was only three years old at the time, but I have a vague memory of my father bringing that shiny belt home," recalls Stasiak's son and former WWE Superstar, Shawn Stasiak. "As a toddler, I thought it was a toy belt. I remember carrying it around the house, playing with it and pretending I was the king of the house."

Unfortunately, playtime lasted only nine days. On December 10, 1973, Bruno Sammartino defeated The Man to reclaim the WWE title. For the Italian strongman, the win made him the first-ever two-time WWE Champion. But for Stasiak, it meant the end of one of the shortest reigns in history.

"It doesn't matter if he held it for nine days, nine seconds, or nine years. He held it and was one of the original WWE Champions. His reign will always be cemented in WWE history," boasts Shawn, whose father passed away in 1997. "I would imagine that he would have liked to have held it longer, or at least on some other occasion, but I'll always remember him referring to it as the happiest nine days of his life. He felt blessed and was very grateful for the opportunity and experience."

By Bruno Sammartino's second WWE title reign, most of the champ's adversaries from the 1960s had either retired or moved on to other promotions, making way for a whole host of new challengers. Despite the fresh faces, however, Sammartino was able to mirror the same success he gained during his first run with the gold.

Ken Patera. Bruiser Brody. Nikolai Volkoff. They all tried to knock off the mighty champion, but all fell short. Stan Hansen came closest in April 1976. While competing at MSG, Hansen lifted Sammartino for a bodyslam, a move he had executed successfully thousands of times in the past. This time, however, the champ's sweaty body caused Hansen to lose his grip, and he dropped Sammartino on his head.

The failed slam broke the champ's neck.

Miraculously, Sammartino continued with the match, despite the injury making him a prime target for Hansen's signature Lariat clothesline. In the end, the referee was forced to stop the match, due to excessive blood loss by Sammartino. Had the official not made the controversial decision, there's a very real chance today's list of WWE Champions would include the name Stan Hansen.

After only two months of rehabilitation, a courageous Bruno Sammartino returned to the ring seeking vengeance. At the second *Showdown* at Shea Stadium, he beat Stan Hansen mercilessly. Eventually, the massacre became too much for the challenger to withstand, and he ran toward the safety of the locker room. Hansen's cowardly act gave Sammartino the count-out win and allowed him to proudly carry the WWE Championship into 1977, his fourteenth calendar year with the gold strapped firmly around his waist.

Bruno Sammartino vs.
Stan Stasiak.

"Superstar"
Billy Graham.

5

A DIFFERENT KIND
OF CHAMPION

By 1977, the image of the ideal WWE Champion had been
set in stone, thanks to the efforts of Bruno Sammartino and
Pedro Morales. For nearly fourteen straight years, fans in the
Northeast knew the champion was somebody worth admiring.

Then came "Superstar" Billy Graham.

With bleached-blond hair, tie-dyed ring attire, and a perfectly chis-eled frame, Graham was unlike anything anyone had ever seen before. Most competitors at this time wore single-colored trunks that rode high enough to cover the bottom of their potbellies. And their interviews were dreadfully predictable and boring. But Graham was none of this. Instead, "Superstar" was a colorfully flamboyant character with unmatched charisma. Influ-enced by boxing great Muhammad Ali, Graham would regularly break out into rhyme, which the fans loved to hate: "I am the man of the hour. The one with the power, too sweet to be sour."

On April 30, 1977, Billy Graham walked into Baltimore's Civic Cen-ter with hopes of ending Bruno Sammartino's nearly three-and-a-half-year WWE Championship reign.

Sammartino was a bit past his prime at this point, but he still fought with the heart of a champion. Now instead of powering through his op-ponents, he was forced to be more creative with his offense. At one point during the match, Sammartino uncharacteristically threw Graham into the ring post. The impact of the move left Graham a bloody mess. Smelling vic-tory, Sammartino continued his onslaught, pounding his challenger with heavy right hands. The blows were so fierce that the referee had no choice but to warn the champion to stop. At that same moment, with Sammar-tino's attention slightly distracted, Graham pulled his opponent's legs from under him. He then pinned the legendary champ's shoulders to the mat, but not before illegally placing his own legs on the top rope for added leverage.

Graham's controversial victory sent the Baltimore crowd into an un-controllable frenzy. Garbage began to fill the ring, as the new WWE Cham-pion made his way toward the protection of the locker room.

Unfortunately for Graham, security was sparse. En route to the back, Superstar was pelted with kicks and punches from the angry mob. In an attempt to protect himself, Graham continually swung his newly won title over his head, hoping it would deter some fans. It didn't.

WWE changed forever on this night. Never before had there been such a showman representing the company as champion. In the years fol-lowing Graham's reign, however, the type of charisma Superstar exhibited practically became a prerequisite, as evidenced by the likes of Hulk Hogan and Ultimate Warrior.

"Superstar"
Billy Graham vs.
Bruno Sammartino.

Fans everywhere were obviously angered by Bruno Sammartino's loss, especially considering the dastardly way in which Superstar pinned their hero. But at least they were able to rest on the thought of Graham quickly losing the gold back to one of their favorites. After all, villains such as Graham never held the title for longer than three weeks.

Superstar battled fan favorite Gorilla Monsoon in his first MSG title defense. Many assumed this was going to be the match in which Graham stumbled. But when that didn't happen, and Superstar arrogantly walked out of the arena with his championship held high, fans finally came to the realization that they weren't going to get the short title reign they had hoped for.

Business began to boom as Graham hit his stride as champion. With his title defenses headlining the card, WWE started setting attendance records at the Boston Garden and Philadelphia Spectrum. With Superstar's name on the marquee, WWE even sold out nineteen of his twenty main events at New York's Madison Square Garden.

Graham's emerging popularity eventually led to title defenses outside of WWE's Northeast territory. He battled Bobo Brazil in Detroit, Dick the Bruiser in St. Louis, Raymond Rougeau in Atlanta; he even traveled to Japan to battle Rusher Kimura in a Steel Cage Match. But it was his fierce rivalry with Florida's Dusty Rhodes that proved most memorable. Their October 1977 Texas Death Match will forever be remembered as one of the most brutal battles of the decade. In the end, it was Graham picking up the win via pinfall, but it was the events prior to the decision that fans remember most about the match. During the encounter, a hundred-foot-long rope was pulled from under the ring. Rhodes grabbed the weapon and wrapped it around Graham's body before draping him over the top ring rope. While gasping for air, the champ stretched his arms wide like a crucifix. Graham, a highly religious man, later said it was an extremely spiritual moment for him.

In January 1978, Billy Graham traveled to Florida to battle Harley Race in a very rare WWE Champion versus NWA Champion best Two-Out-of-Three Falls Match. Both men were villains at the time, but the crowd in Miami's Orange Bowl strongly backed Race, largely because his NWA affiliation gave him more exposure in the Sunshine State than Graham. To

Bob Backlund vs. "Superstar" Billy Graham.

ensure the match would be called down the middle, both organizations sent special referees. Gorilla Monsoon represented WWE, while Don Curtis did the job for the NWA. Mother Nature also played a major role in the historic encounter, as rain poured throughout the night, causing both Graham and Race to slip and slide all over the ring.

Superstar won the first fall, utilizing his rib-crunching bear hug. The second fall went to Race following a suplex. During the third and deciding fall, Race locked a sleeper hold on Graham. The move dropped the WWE Champion to the mat, where Race went for the cover.

There were now just three seconds separating the NWA from bragging rights over WWE. The count began: one . . . two . . . and that was it. Just milliseconds before the three count could be made, the bell rang, ending the contest. The sixty-minute time-limit had expired.

Billy Graham returned to New York with his WWE Championship strapped securely around his waist. About this time, fans began to recognize Superstar for the great entertainer he truly was. The boos miraculously started turning into cheers, despite Graham's natural villainous actions. And fans began to hang on his every word, almost the same way they responded to The Rock two decades later.

With an MSG crowd firmly behind him, Graham defended the WWE Championship against Mil Mascaras in early 1978. In typical Superstar fashion, he attempted to pin his challenger while utilizing the ring ropes for leverage. Bob Backlund, who was in Mascaras's corner that night, spotted the injustice and attacked the champ. It was this one moment that eventually led to a match that would send Graham into a downward spiral from which he almost never recovered.

After Backlund attacked Graham, Vince McMahon Sr. set up a WWE Championship contest between the two men. Superstar heavily objected, claiming a "boring" competitor such as Backlund had no business in the ring with the champ. Graham's pleas ultimately fell on deaf ears. Many believed McMahon wanted more of an All-American boy representing his company as champion, and Backlund certainly fit that bill, and was granted the Championship Match.

In protest to having to defend his title against Bob Backlund, Billy Graham walked to the ring wearing all white that night—a far cry from his normal over-the-top garb. The subtle protest, however, did very little to help him in the ring. Following an atomic drop, Backlund covered Graham for the three count.

Ironically, Superstar's reign ended the same way it had begun: with his foot on the rope. Normally, this would break the referee's count. But the official that night failed to spot it, effectively making February 20, 1978, the final day of Billy Graham's ten-month WWE Championship reign.

6

ALL-AMERICAN BOY

Unlike "Superstar" Billy Graham, Bob Backlund wasn't about running his mouth or arrogantly flaunting his title. Instead, the Minnesota native was more of a silent assassin. At first, wrestling fans found it difficult to switch gears to a more vanilla brand of champion ... but in time they found it hard not to appreciate his in-ring athletic prowess and boy-next-door good looks.

Backlund's first test as champion came mere days after defeating Graham. With company pride on the line, he squared off against NWA Champion Harley Race in a rare Winner-Take-All title match. In the end, a sixty-minute time-limit draw prevented either championship from switching owners. Over the next few years, Backlund confidently represented WWE several more times, battling other outside champions such as Nick Bockwinkel (AWA) and Ric Flair (NWA).

Within WWE, Bob Backlund was faced with equally superior competition. Athletes like Don Muraco, Sgt. Slaughter, George "The Animal" Steele, and Ken Patera all tried to take the champ down. But with manager Arnold Skaaland by his side, Backlund was a tough man to beat.

In November 1979, one competitor proved skilled enough to pin the champ's shoulders to the mat. While on tour in Japan, Bob Backlund found himself on the losing end of a thrilling title defense against the great Antonio Inoki. While on the same tour, Backlund cashed in his rematch clause and regained the gold. The contest, however, was marred by outside interference, causing WWE President Hisashi Shinma to void Backlund's win and give the title back to Inoki. Being the proud competitor that he was, the Japanese legend refused to accept the gift in such a nonathletic manner. As a result, the WWE Championship was temporarily vacated.

Back in the United States, Backlund won yet another match to reclaim the title. Considering the gold found its way back around Backlund's waist, as well as the controversies surrounding the series of matches in Japan, WWE ultimately chose not to recognize Inoki's victory.

By 1983, Bob Backlund had distinguished himself as the second-longest-reigning champion of all time, an accomplishment that still holds true today. Around the same time, Vincent K. McMahon had purchased WWE from his father. The younger McMahon had aspirations of taking his new property global, which would eventually lead to Backlund's downfall. The highly-motivated promoter began injecting his roster with larger-than-life personalities that drew the attention of fans worldwide. Within months, names like "Rowdy" Roddy Piper, Jesse "The Body" Ventura, and Hulk Hogan all became international sensations. And with each new name that was added to the roster, it became increasingly more clear that the All-American Boy was going to have a tough time keeping up with the fresh faces.

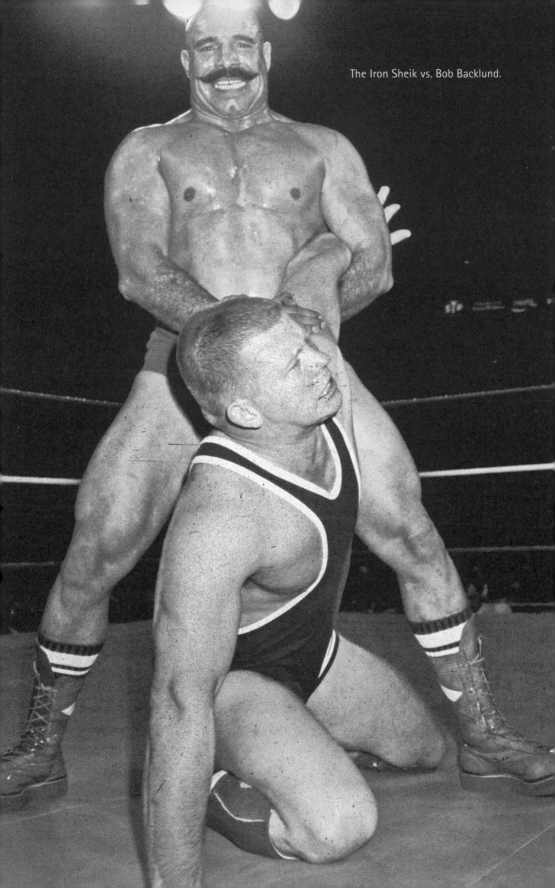

The Iron Sheik vs. Bob Backlund.

Backlund knew that all the new Superstars walking around the WWE locker room represented a nearly impossible challenge for him; but after nearly six years with the gold, he refused to stick his head in the sand. Instead, he chose to proudly defend against any of the most capable newcomers. One of the first to step forward was former AWA competitor the Iron Sheik.

One week prior to his showdown with the Iranian Superstar, Bob Backlund agreed to participate in a Persian Club challenge. That seemingly safe decision ultimately led to his undoing. During the challenge, the Sheik viciously attacked Backlund from behind, hitting him about the neck and shoulder region with the oversized clubs. With just days remaining before their title match at Madison Square Garden, some questioned if Backlund would be able to compete. But being the fighting champion that he was, on December 26, 1983, Backlund defended the WWE Championship against the Iron Sheik.

Moments before the match officially got under way, the Sheik again attacked Backlund from behind, targeting his injured left side. The assault gave the challenger an advantage he never relinquished. For the next ten minutes, Sheik shouted "Iran number one," while systematically attacking Backlund's injury. Finally, the challenger attempted to put the champ out of his misery by applying his patented Camel Clutch.

Bob Backlund refused to quit, despite the excruciating havoc being wreaked on his neck and back. The champ screamed out in pain, while the Iron Sheik responded with more and more pressure. Realizing his man was risking permanent injury, manager Arnold Skaaland made the difficult decision to throw the towel into the ring, signifying the end of the match, as well as Bob Backlund's nearly six-year WWE Championship reign.

"It was a big pleasure to me because I was the first Middle Easterner to win the championship," boasts the Iron Sheik, more than twenty-five years later. "I came from Tehran, Iran, to America and became champion. That was the biggest honor for me, as well as for all my country people and all my wrestling fans in America."

The proud Sheik carried his title into 1984, when he successfully defended against Chief Jay Strongbow and Tito Santana. But before his reign could gain any serious traction, he was quickly thrown into a title defense against another former AWA competitor: Hulk Hogan.

7

HULKAMANIA

Many of today's fans recognize Hulk Hogan as the Babe Ruth of WWE, the Superstar who helped revolutionize sports-entertainment and turned it into the global phenomenon it is today. But that success didn't come overnight for the Hulkster. In fact, he spent many years stumbling before finally perfecting his persona in the mid-1980s.

Following several lackluster years on the independent scene during the late 1970s, Terry "The Hulk" Boulder considered quitting altogether to go work on the docks. Before he was able to hang up his boots for good, however, legendary wrestler Terry Funk urged him to give Vince McMahon Sr. a call.

Heading into the conversation, the six-foot-eight Superstar had very little intention of going to work for McMahon. But by the end of the call, the persistent promoter convinced Hulk to pack up and leave Tampa for the bright lights of New York and WWE. When he arrived, McMahon dropped "Terry Boulder" from his name and added the surname "Hogan." This added some Irish to WWE's globalized roster, which also included Italians (Bruno Sammartino), Poles (Ivan Putski), Native Americans (Chief Jay Strongbow), and Latinos (Pedro Morales).

Working as a villain, Hogan saw his career begin to take off, especially after competing against the legendary Andre the Giant and spending some time in New Japan Pro Wrestling, a Japanese-based promotion McMahon worked with on a regular basis. He became so popular, in fact, that Hollywood came calling. Looking for an oversized athlete to play the role of Thunderlips in *Rocky III*, Sylvester Stallone asked the Hulkster if he would be interested. An excited Hogan agreed and ran back to tell McMahon the news.

"If you leave to do the *Rocky* movie, you'll never work for this company again," McMahon said, according to the 2002 autobiography, *Hollywood Hulk Hogan*.

McMahon had plans for Hogan that conflicted with the movie's shooting schedule, but the starry-eyed Superstar did the film anyway. And as promised, after his ten days of shooting wrapped, he was left without a job. An unemployed Hogan questioned if he would ever set foot inside a ring again. Then, in an act of desperation, he sent a promotional photo from the movie to American Wrestling Association promoter Verne Gagne.

The AWA was interested and Hogan made his debut in 1981. Over the next few years, he experienced great success and even greater frustration. The wins were easy to come by for Hogan; it was the behind-the-scenes politics that angered him. According to Hogan, Gagne demanded a percentage of the money the Hulkster was making from his frequent trips to Japan.

Gagne also began selling T-shirts with Hogan's likeness on them, without giving the Superstar a portion of the profits. On top of all this, Hogan claims Gagne was pushing his daughter Kathy on him, with the hope that she could prevent him from leaving the AWA.

By 1983, Hogan had enough of the politics. So when WWE came calling again, he jumped at the opportunity. By this time, Vince McMahon Jr. was in charge and he was looking for a charismatic big man to help him lead his regional company toward its goal of national, then global, dominance.

Hogan's sudden departure from the AWA greatly angered Gagne. He knew that with the Hulkster in the fold, WWE's chances of expanding into his Minnesota territory and beyond just increased exponentially. But he wasn't going to sit idly by and let McMahon overtake his territory. Instead, when he found out that the Iron Sheik was going to defend his title against Hogan, he came up with a plan.

"My coach, Mr. Verne Gagne, called me before my match with Mr. Hulk Hogan," recalls the Iron Sheik, regarding his January 1984 title defense. "He said to me, 'My company is going to go down now that Hogan is in [WWE]. Do me a favor because I am going to go bankrupt. Don't drop the belt to Hogan. Instead, break his legs and come back home to Minnesota. I will give you $100,000.' "

But the Sheik never thought twice about taking the money. "It didn't matter if it was $100,000 or $100,000,000, I have too much respect for WWE. It would have been very easy for me to break Hulk Hogan's legs, but I'm a businessman."

Instead, the Sheik marched into the McMahon office at Madison Square Garden and told both Sr. and Jr. the news. According to the Sheik, a very appreciative McMahon Sr. hugged the WWE Champion and told him how much he appreciated his loyalty.

"God bless him," says the Iron Sheik of Vince McMahon Sr. "He was a great promoter for me and it was a huge honor to work for him. He was a good man."

Filled with pride for his company, the Iron Sheik entered the ring at MSG prepared to defend his WWE Championship against newcomer Hogan. Unfortunately for the Sheik, destiny was not on his side this night.

The Iron Sheik vs. Hulk Hogan.

The Hulkster destroyed the champ in less than six minutes to capture the WWE title.

After the match, the Sheik walked into Hogan's locker room to fill him in on Gagne's failed hit.

"He hugged me and he kissed me," recalls the Sheik. "He said to me, 'Sheiky baby, I owe you one.' But he forgot all about it later on."

Despite his superior wrestling skills, the Iron Sheik failed to reach full main event status again, something he blames on the American hostage crisis in Iran.

"I was the hottest thing in the Big Apple. I was the hottest human being on the earth," boasts the Sheik. "I was rare because I was a shooter and All-American three-time AAU champion. I sold out everywhere. If not for the hostage situation, I would have been on top of the card longer. But a lot of people threatened me and wanted to kill me. People waited outside the arena. [WWE] had to bring me down because people threatened to damage me. I think if not for the hostage situation, probably I be champion longer."

While the Iron Sheik slipped down to midcard level, Hogan set sail on one of the most influential periods in sports-entertainment history. Within months, WWE became the hottest ticket in whatever town they went to, and not just with the fans, but celebrities too. It wasn't uncommon to see Sean Connery or Regis Philbin or Donald Trump enjoying a WWE event from the front row. WWE even won over Grammy Award–winning Best New Artist Cyndi Lauper, who took her fandom to a whole new level when she became the manager of female wrestler Wendi Richter. As a result of the celebrity involvement, the false pretense that wrestling was only low culture began to disappear. Suddenly, being a WWE fan became vogue.

Even *Sports Illustrated* stood up and took notice. The then-leader in sports journalism featured Hulk Hogan on the cover in April 1985–the first time ever for an active wrestler.

With Hulk Hogan as champion, WWE kept getting hotter. After a year of selling out every arena they played, McMahon decided he needed a marquee event where he could showcase WWE to an entire nation watching on closed-circuit television. He dubbed the event *WrestleMania*.

Nearly three decades later, *WrestleMania* has solidified itself as the crown jewel of sports-entertainment. In 1985, however, the event proved

to be a financial risk. Between the marketing, celebrity appearance fees, television production, and everything else that went into producing a mega event, McMahon was putting the entire future of his company on the line with this one show. But behind the power of *Hulkamania*, the event became a resounding success. With *Rocky III* costar Mr. T as his tag team partner, Hogan was able to send the sell-out MSG crowd home happy by defeating "Rowdy" Roddy Piper and Paul Orndorff.

Over the next several years, Hogan turned back the game's top names to maintain his firm grasp on the WWE Championship. "Cowboy" Bob Orton, Greg "The Hammer" Valentine, Terry Funk, and Don Muraco tried to knock him off his perch, but all failed. He even toppled much larger Superstars, such as King Kong Bundy (at *WrestleMania 2*) and Big John Studd.

Hogan was awarded a gigantic trophy to help celebrate his third straight year as WWE Champion. Around the same time, to celebrate his fifteen-year undefeated streak, close friend Andre the Giant was also recognized with a trophy, albeit a considerably smaller one. When Andre was presented with the award, an excited Hulkster came out to celebrate with his buddy. Andre, however, saw Hogan's involvement as an attempt to steal the spotlight, so he walked out midceremony.

Andre's disappearing act during the trophy presentation eventually led to a showdown with Hulk Hogan at *WrestleMania III*. In front of a record 93,173 screaming fans at the Pontiac Silverdome in Michigan, Hogan stood eye-to-chin with his former friend, awaiting the start of his toughest challenge to date. Andre made the first move, shoving the champ. Hogan quickly responded

with a shove of his own, followed by three right hands. An overconfident Hulkster then went for a bodyslam, but Andre's massive frame was too much for the champ to handle, resulting in more than 500 pounds crashing down on Hogan. The ref immediately dropped to his knees to make what appeared to be the match-ending three count. Miraculously, though, Hogan was able to lift his shoulder from the mat just as the official was completing the count. The call could have gone either way, but the referee ultimately decided that the match would continue. The decision to go on remains one of the most controversial in WWE Championship history.

Undeterred by his failed bodyslam attempt, Hogan went for the same move later in the contest. This time he executed it perfectly. With Andre felled, the champ bounced off the ropes and hit his famous legdrop for the win. After the match, tears of joy fell from Hulk Hogan's eyes, as he held his title high in celebration.

Despite his epic victory over Andre at *WrestleMania III*, Hogan was far from finished with his former friend. Following a disappointing outing against the Giant's *Survivor Series* team on Thanksgiving, the champ agreed to once again defend the title against Andre. This time, however, there was a money-laden twist.

Since arriving in WWE in 1987, Ted DiBiase was on a quest to prove that everybody had a price for the Million Dollar Man. He would pluck fans from the audience and make them bark like a dog or shine his shoes just for a few bucks. After a few weeks of picking on fans, DiBiase set his sights higher when he offered Hogan a life-changing sum of money in exchange for the WWE Championship.

A few weeks passed with no answer from the Hulkster, leading many to believe he might actually take the offer. In reality, he was simply toying with DiBiase. His answer was exactly what every *Hulkamaniac* wanted it to be: "Hell no!"

The rejection forced DiBiase to come up with Plan B, which consisted of finding a Superstar skilled enough to defeat Hogan and immoral enough to turn around and sell the title to the Million Dollar Man. DiBiase's target accomplice: Andre the Giant.

"That whole story was one of the best in history," remembers DiBiase.

"It was the launching point for the Million Dollar Man character. Here I am, this over-the-top, arrogant, rich guy whose god was money. So the ultimate in arrogance for me was to say, 'I'm going to go out there and buy the title; I'm not going to win it.' Of course, all the fans were shocked at the audacity of the Million Dollar Man. They said, 'You can't buy the championship, it's impossible.' "

But it was. And just to make sure, he also bought a referee.

Dave Hebner was the assigned official for the Hogan-Andre rematch. But prior to the contest, DiBiase had him abducted and locked in a backroom. He then sent out an identical referee whom he had bought off. Throughout the entire contest, nobody realized that it wasn't Dave Hebner calling the action.

Late in the match, Andre executed a rather pedestrian suplex on Hogan and went for the pin. The faux ref dropped to the mat and made the three count, despite the Hulkster successfully getting his shoulder up off the mat after the one count.

Hogan immediately jumped to his feet and began protesting with the referee. But it was too late. The championship had already been handed to Andre, marking the end of Hogan's amazing four-year reign.

As promised, the Giant gave the gold to DiBiase only moments after being announced as champion. Then, like a group of thieves in the night, the Million Dollar Man and his crew ran off, leaving Hogan in the ring to try and make sense of what had just happened.

A flabbergasted Hulkster finally began to put the pieces together when Dave Hebner, who had freed himself from backstage captivity, ran to the ring and confronted his look-alike. It was at this moment that Hulk realized that DiBiase's camp had bought the referee. Filled with rage, Hogan lifted the evil official and tossed him out of the ring and up the aisle.

"I ran down and tried to catch the ref," recalls former WWE official Tim White. "But the adrenaline took over and Hogan launched him well over our heads. The only thing I could do was look up and wave good-bye. He missed us by about fifteen feet, landed on the floor, and broke a couple of ribs."

More than 15,000 fans walked out of Market Square Arena in Indianapolis that night with their heads low. The apparent new champ, Ted DiBiase, and Andre the Giant, however, left with a reason to rejoice.

"I celebrated that night," says DiBiase. "I went out with the guys closest to me. Obviously, Andre was there, and if you went out with Andre, you can guarantee that there would be some drinking going on.

"But what I remember more is the private moment in my hotel room. I remember thinking very much of my dad [Wrestler "Iron" Mike DiBiase] and missing him, wishing he could be there to see what was going on with his son. I remember opening my bag and pulling that title out. It took me back to the time when my dad came off the road and as a kid I would always open up his bag and air out his shoes and throw his dirty stuff in the laundry. And whenever he had a championship, I would go in the bag and look at the title and think to myself, 'One day, one day it will be me.' And then it was."

Actually, it wasn't. Days after Andre handed the title over to DiBiase, WWE President Jack Tunney reviewed the rulebook and made the following announcement:

> The decision of the referee is, as always, unfortunately, final. Therefore, Hulk Hogan is not the [WWE] Champion. However, it clearly states in the rulebook, that in order for a wrestler to be deemed champion, he must either pin the reigning titleholder or make him submit. That is the only way a wrestler can become champion. Therefore, unequivocally, I can state that Ted DiBiase is also *not* the [WWE] Champion. Furthermore, it also clearly states in the rulebook that a reigning champion may at any time in his tenure, end his reign by publicly surrendering the title, which is exactly what happened when Andre the Giant presented the championship belt to Ted DiBiase. Therefore, Andre is also *not* the champion either. It is my decision that to be fair to the last two reigning champions of record, Hogan and Andre, and to furthermore be fair with the number-one contenders who would have faced either Andre or Hogan as champion, I now declare the title vacant.

8

THE MEGA-POWERS EXPLODE

Jack Tunney's decision to vacate the title marked the first time in WWE's twenty-five-year history that there was no champion. To fill the vacancy, the president ordered a fourteen-man tournament to take place in March 1988 at *WrestleMania IV*. As the two most recent titlists, Andre the

Giant and Hulk Hogan were scheduled to face each other, but not before receiving automatic byes into the quarterfinals. Amazingly, the built-in advantage did little to help them regain the gold; both Superstars were disqualified after blatant use of a steel chair.

With Andre and Hogan no longer in the title hunt, Ted DiBiase and "Macho Man" Randy Savage advanced to the finals with relative ease. Prior to the start of the match, special guest ring announcer Bob Uecker had the honor of introducing each Superstar. The Million Dollar Man made his way to the ring first to very little fanfare. In 1988, it was still common for Superstars to walk to the ring sans entrance themes. DiBiase at the time was one of those Superstars who practiced very little pageantry.

Savage was the anti-DiBiase. Once his signature theme song—"Pomp and Circumstance"—rang out from the Trump Plaza loudspeakers, the capacity crowd erupted, making it nearly impossible to hear Uecker's intro-

duction. When Savage and his manager, Miss Elizabeth, finally emerged from the dressing room area, they were wearing a different ring robe and dress than earlier. It was their fourth wardrobe change of the night.

"He didn't want to rob people of seeing him for the first time, even if it was the fourth. He took this aspect of the business very seriously," says Savage's brother, former WWE Superstar Lanny Poffo. "He didn't believe the match started when the bell rang, he believed the match started when the dressing room door opened. He spent a lot of money on those robes."

Savage was, indeed, a superior showman outside the ring. Once the bell rang, however, he was all business—something the Million Dollar Man found out the hard way. By match's end, he found himself victimized by a Macho Man flying elbow drop. The move effectively ended DiBiase's dreams of becoming a legitimate WWE Champion.

Savage's victory marked the culmination of an eighteen-year journey. Making the moment even more special was the fact that he got to share it with his real-life love, Elizabeth. He also shared the spotlight with Hulk Hogan, who joined the couple in celebrating the victory. As a result, the lasting image of *WrestleMania IV* will forever be Savage holding Elizabeth on his shoulder while Hogan stands nearby pointing at the celebratory couple.

Hulk remained by the new champ's side for many more months following *WrestleMania IV*. Known as the Mega-Powers, Hogan and Savage formed a union that struck fear into WWE's most formidable Superstars. The only tandem they failed to impress were the Mega-Bucks (DiBiase and

Randy Savage and Miss Elizabeth.

Andre), who confidently agreed to battle the champ and his partner in the first-ever *SummerSlam* main event.

Just as they promised, DiBiase and Andre owned much of the match's momentum. But just when it looked like they were going to pick up the win via count-out, Elizabeth climbed to the ring apron and removed her skirt to reveal a very skimpy red undergarment. By 1988 standards, the mini strip-tease proved to be quite risqué, and it also worked to distract the Mega-Bucks and special guest referee Jesse Ventura. Hogan and Savage used the distraction to climb back into the ring and dispose of Andre. Macho Man then landed a flying elbow drop on the Million Dollar Man, which was followed by a Hogan legdrop for the win.

The sold-out Madison Square Garden crowd roared as the victors celebrated. In an act of unadulterated jubilation, the Hulkster grabbed Miss Elizabeth and gave her a gigantic hug. Savage spotted the embrace and looked on quizzically, but he eventually shrugged it off and continued to celebrate.

Hogan kept getting closer to Elizabeth as the new year approached. With each passing month, he continued to make what Savage saw as questionable advances toward the beautiful manager, but the champ let each one slide. Finally, in February 1989, Macho Man had enough.

During a tag team encounter with the Twin Towers, a fed-up Savage slapped Hulk Hogan across the face before ultimately walking out of the match, effectively ending their nearly year-long union. To help further drive home the point that the Mega-Powers were done, Savage attacked Hogan in the locker-room area after the match. This final exclamation point helped put the wheels in motion for Hogan and Savage's epic encounter at *WrestleMania V*.

For the only time in WWE history, the same venue played host to back-to-back *WrestleMania* shows when Trump Plaza was selected as the site for the fifth annual event. Thirteen matches made up the event's undercard, and while each offered great intrigue, none were as heavily anticipated as the main event: Randy Savage versus Hulk Hogan for the WWE Championship.

Midway through the match, referee Earl Hebner deemed Elizabeth's presence at ringside too distracting to the competitors, so he ejected her from the arena. With the beautiful manager out of the way, Savage and Hogan were left to decide which Superstar was the better man minus any

outside distractions. In the end, the Hulkster proved to be too much for the Macho Man. With a boot to the face, followed by a trademark legdrop, Hogan put an end to Savage's epic year-long WWE Championship reign. In the nearly twenty years that followed, such great names as Bret Hart, Shawn Michaels, and Stone Cold Steve Austin went on to capture the WWE title. But none were able to hold it as long as Randy Savage. It wouldn't be until John Cena in 2007 that the title stayed around a single waist for more than a year.

Hogan's victory over Savage made him only the second man to hold the WWE Championship on more than one occasion (Bruno Sammartino was the other). It also helped catapult his career back to the silver screen.

In June 1989, Vince McMahon teamed with New Line Cinema to produce *No Holds Barred*, a major motion picture starring the WWE Champion. Hogan was cast to play the role of Rip, a popular Superstar who must prevent an evil consortium from killing his friends. Rip ultimately foils the dastardly plan when he defeats chief antagonist Zeus, who was played by Tommy "Tiny" Lister.

Despite the happy ending, *No Holds Barred* failed at the box office. It also spawned a large level of animosity between stars Hogan and Zeus, which eventually bled over to WWE arenas. Over the next several months, the Hulkster teamed with longtime friend Brutus "The Barber" Beefcake to systematically dismantle any hopes Zeus had of becoming a fulltime professional wrestler.

While Hogan was successfully turning back Zeus, a new force was beginning to gain favor with WWE fans. After defeating the Honky Tonk Man in record time to capture the Intercontinental Championship in August, Ultimate Warrior saw a great spike in popularity. For the next several months, fans were able to turn on their TVs with great confidence, knowing that their two favorite heroes were in complete control of WWE's singles titles. But as 1990 approached, it was becoming apparent that there was only room at the top for one megastar. Hogan and Warrior were on a collision course. A battle between the two Superstars was inevitable, and only one event could host such a dream match: *WrestleMania*.

Hulk Hogan vs. Ultimate Warrior, *WrestleMania VI*.

9

PASSING THE TORCH

WWE took its grandest show north of the border in 1990 when Toronto's newly opened SkyDome became the first-ever venue outside of the United States to host a *Wrestle-Mania*. The event also marked another significant first: Prior to the show, President Jack Tunney announced that both Hulk

Hogan's WWE Championship and Ultimate Warrior's Intercontinental Championship would be on the line in the main event. Never before had so much been at stake in one match.

Realizing the magnitude of the contest, both Superstars showed up in tremendous physical condition. They engaged in a game of one-upmanship in the match's earliest moments, complete with an inconclusive test of strength and an ineffective shoulder block that resulted in announcer Gorilla Monsoon uttering his famous phrase, "the irresistible force meeting the immovable object."

As the match raged on, Hogan fought off a Warrior splash to gain the upper hand. Smelling victory, the Hulkster landed his popular big boot and bounced off the ropes for the legdrop. But Warrior was able to move out of the way before the champ could slam his massive limb down. With a shocked Hogan lying on the mat, Warrior whipped off the ropes and connected with another big splash. This time it was enough to keep the Hulkster down for a three count, thus ending his second reign on top, which fell just one day short of lasting a full year.

With tears in his eyes, Hogan grabbed the WWE Championship from the ringside timekeeper and walked into the ring. A hush fell over the Sky-Dome crowd as they tried to predict in their minds what the former champ was going to do with the title. Many assumed the upset loser was going to whack Warrior with the gold. But Hogan proved them all wrong. With his chin up, the Hulkster handed the championship over to the new titlist before giving him an emotional embrace. Unlike Randy Savage's victory at *WrestleMania IV*, Hogan then left the ring to let Warrior have his moment. On his way out, he gave the new champ the now-famous salute. At the time, many saw the gesture as a symbolic passing of the torch.

Ultimate Warrior's popularity reached even greater heights following his *WrestleMania VI* victory over Hogan. His unmatched energy, chiseled frame, psychedelic face paint, and repertoire of high-impact maneuvers helped make him a household name; it wasn't long before kids started showing up at arenas with paint-covered faces in support of their offbeat hero.

In typical Warrior fashion, the popular new champion made quick work of Haku and Ted DiBiase. He then toppled Rick Rude in a *Summer-*

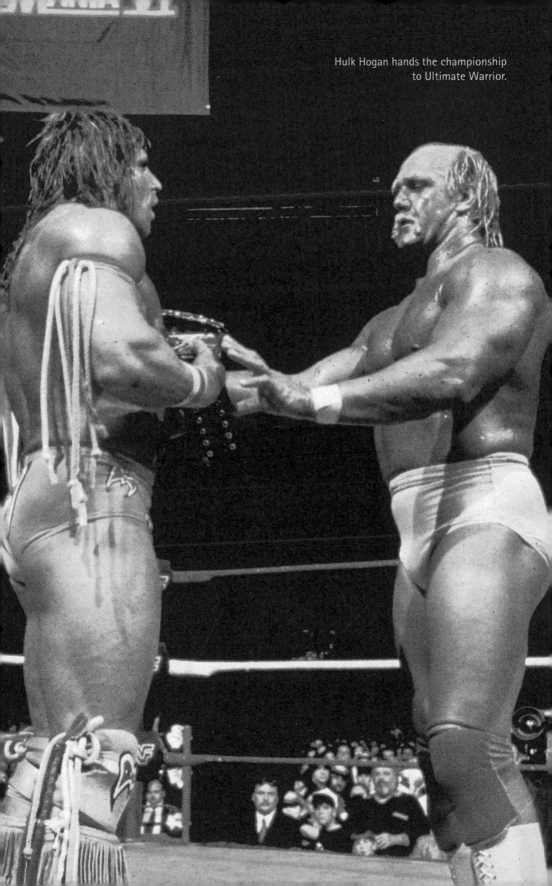
Hulk Hogan hands the championship to Ultimate Warrior.

Slam Steel Cage Match before uncharacteristically granting the Million Dollar Man another title opportunity, despite handily defeating him earlier in his reign. Warrior was able to walk away from the match with the disqualification victory, but it was the events that followed that proved most costly.

While Warrior was celebrating his victory, "Macho King" Randy Savage ran to the ring and attacked the champ with his royal scepter. The assault set off one of the most unique rivalries of all time—a rivalry that eventually cost Warrior the gold, despite his never officially stepping into the ring with Savage.

Over the next several months, Savage became a thorn in the champion's side. A major showdown between the two Superstars looked inevitable, but along the way, Macho King suffered an injury that prevented him from in-ring competition. The fans never learned of Savage's setback; instead he kept it under wraps, hoping it would quickly heal while he still had Warrior's attention.

With Savage temporarily out of the WWE Championship picture, one Superstar stepped up and took full advantage of the opening. To some, he seemed like the most unlikely of challengers. But for Sgt. Slaughter, it was about being in the right place at the right time.

10

USA, USA

In the summer of 1984, Sgt. Slaughter used his heated rivalry with the hated Iron Sheik to become an American hero. Filled with pride, fans flocked to New York's Madison Square Garden to watch the larger-than-life former Marine Corps member take it to WWE's greatest villain.

Recognizing Slaughter's increasing popularity, the Hasbro toy company approached the Superstar about becoming a real-life G.I. Joe. Up to this point, all the characters in G.I. Joe were fictitious. Hasbro saw Slaughter as somebody who could travel the country and serve as a spokesperson on behalf of the popular toy line. As part of the deal, he would be inserted into the popular cartoon series and be given his own action figure.

The thought of becoming a real-life G.I. Joe was appealing to Slaughter. His boss, Vince McMahon Jr., however, saw the opportunity as a conflict to his responsibility as a Superstar. As a result, Slaughter was forced to choose between G.I. Joe and WWE. At the height of his in-ring popularity, he surprisingly chose G.I. Joe.

Slaughter spent the next five years working with Hasbro. Though risky at first, the move ultimately proved to be beneficial, as the exposure he gained, coupled with his prior success against the Iron Sheik, made him a household name. People everywhere—not just wrestling or G.I. Joe fans— recognized Sgt. Slaughter as a true American hero.

After his contract with Hasbro ended, Slaughter received a call from McMahon. "Are you ready to come back to work?" he was asked. "Come to my house tomorrow. I have an idea for you."

As an excited Slaughter hung up the phone, thoughts of WWE taking his patriotic persona to even greater heights began to run through his head. He sat down with his family that night and told them about his upcoming meeting at McMahon's house. Collectively, they began to think of ways to celebrate Slaughter's return to the ring.

"When I got to the house, Vince had the complete opposite idea," says Slaughter. "He wanted to make me the worst bad guy of all time. He wanted me to side with Saddam Hussein as an Iraqi sympathizer and look at Americans as weak."

With the Persian Gulf War looming, the idea of Sgt. Slaughter denouncing his country would certainly send fans into a frenzy. So McMahon urged the Superstar to speak to his family before making any decisions, considering a villainous Slaughter would undoubtedly impact more than just the man inside the ring. At first, his loved ones thought he was crazy . . . but Slaughter reminded them that anything can happen in WWE.

"So we went for it. In the early goings, I really destroyed all my opponents. At the same time, the Ultimate Puke and Randy Savage were fighting

Sgt. Slaughter vs. Ultimate Warrior.

over the WWE Championship, but Randy got injured. That's when Vince came to me out of nowhere and told me I was going to take Randy's place against Ultimate Warrior."

The match took place at the 1991 *Royal Rumble*. Clad in red, white, and blue, Warrior dominated Slaughter throughout the majority of the contest. But just when it looked like he was going to put Slaughter away for good, Randy Savage ran to ringside and smacked Warrior over the head with his scepter behind the ref's back. Slaughter then dropped an elbow on his opponent for good measure before covering him for the win.

Shocked, the crowd in Miami barely reacted. There was a part of them who hoped Savage's interference would cause a disqualification. But it didn't. Several anxious moments passed before ring announcer Howard Finkel finally made the announcement: "Ladies and gentlemen, here is the official decision. The winner of this bout . . . and *new* World Wrestling Federation Champion . . . Sgt. Slaughter."

The Miami Arena nearly rioted, as the new champ was showered with jeers.

"At that moment, I knew I had done my job well," recalls Slaughter. "I had a tremendous match with somebody who couldn't have that good a match. I just stood there holding the title in the air, listening to all the boos."

"This is an outrage!" screamed legendary play-by-play man Gorilla Monsoon, and fans across America agreed. But behind the scenes, nearly one hundred percent of the locker room rejoiced. Not because an Iraqi sympathizer had won the title—but because Ultimate Warrior had finally lost it.

TED DIBIASE ON WARRIOR'S REIGN: The one title switch that upset me was Hogan to Warrior because he was one guy that didn't deserve it. The greatest thing Warrior had going for him was his body. It almost ends there. If you listen to his interviews, none of them made any sense. Every night, he got in there and did the same thing— his music played, he ran to the ring, shook the ropes, and before you knew it, it was over. He was a guy who had the title and never appreciated it. He was given a gift, and then he tried to hold the company up for more money. The guy's just a jerk. If you look at the list of WWE Champions, there aren't too many guys that I would say were not deserving of being there. Warrior did not deserve to be there. We definitely celebrated after he lost.

Meanwhile, Sgt. Slaughter immediately went back to work, recording interviews and taking photos until three o'clock in the morning. When the new champ finally left the arena, he and his agent stopped for something to eat before going to the hotel. The restaurant was empty, with the exception of the chef. Slaughter and his agent sat patiently while waiting for service. After nearly fifteen minutes had passed, the agent leaned over to the chef and asked if they could order.

"You can eat. *He* can't," said the chef, pointing at Slaughter. Proudly sporting a Marine Corps tattoo, he proceeded to tell the agent that he had seen the *Royal Rumble* and didn't care if Slaughter was the WWE Champion or not—he wasn't going to serve an American turncoat.

So Slaughter went back to his hotel room hungry. Once there, he pulled his newly won title out of his bag. "It was kind of a purple violet color, of all colors," remembers Slaughter. "Not the type of championship you want to walk around with. But that's what Ultimate Warrior wanted. He demanded it be that color. I looked up to the heavens and said to myself, 'Thank you, Lord.' Everything I worked so hard for, all the times being away from my family on holidays and birthdays and anniversaries, it all finally made some sense when I was sitting there holding the belt. I then started thinking about all the great champions who came before me. I knew my name was going to be a part of history with some of the greatest in professional wrestling."

The next day, Sgt. Slaughter was on top of the world as he walked into the arena. He arrived fairly early and before he could even unpack his bags, Chief Jay Strongbow ran over to ask if he had talked to his wife yet.

"No," Slaughter replied.

"Have you talked to Vince?"

"No. What's the problem?"

Strongbow failed to reply before hurrying off. Slaughter could tell something wasn't right. He immediately called his wife, but there was no answer. Now Slaughter started to worry. Finally, he got hold of Vince McMahon.

"Somebody called and threatened to kill you, kill me, kill our families, blow up the office, and blow up our homes," McMahon told Slaughter. "As a precaution, I called your wife and asked her if there was someplace she could spend the night until I could get some security at your home."

Vince McMahon held true to his promise. When Slaughter finally got home ten days later, he found a Winnebago parked in his driveway and four security guards walking the perimeter of his property. Not quite sure what to think of the situation, Slaughter walked over to the men.

"I introduced myself and they showed me that they were packing weapons. They told me we would be protected at all times. They said they would take my children to school and pick them up. They drove my wife to the mall or wherever she wanted to go. It didn't sit well with her at the time—she didn't want anybody with guns taking her kids to school or her to the supermarket."

Despite the threat, Slaughter not only continued to support Iraq each week on television, but he turned up the heat even more. Alongside General Adnan, who had actually gone to college with Saddam Hussein, Slaughter would pull different stunts every night in an attempt to rile up the crowd. One night they brought out a cake and asked the crowd to sing "Happy Birthday" to Saddam. The next they forced the ring announcer to read a written statement claiming it was Veterans Day in Iraq and Sgt. Slaughter wanted everybody to stand and pay their respects to the Iraqi soldiers who died in the takeover of Kuwait. Each night, an explosion of hate would pour down on the WWE Champion. And he loved every minute of it.

With each new stunt came a new threat. It seemed like every city Slaughter set foot in threatened his life. But he refused to let it deter his success.

"One time in Philadelphia, a lady called the police and told them that her son was going to the wrestling matches and was going to kill me. They came and told me that there was a possibility somebody in the audience may try to harm me. They said I had the right not to go out there if I didn't want to. I talked to the road agents and [Arnold] Skaaland and told them I was going to go out there and do my job." No incident occurred during the match.

A similar situation happened in New Jersey. Luckily, they found the suspect, who was carrying a gun, before any harm could be done. This threat sparked the FBI to meet with the WWE Champion before a show at

Hulk Hogan celebrates
the defeat of Sgt. Slaughter.

Madison Square Garden. They took him into a quiet room in the back and advised him to wear a bulletproof vest while wrestling. He wore it for a few weeks before ultimately deciding it wasn't for him.

Nearly two decades later, a brave Slaughter never recalls actually feeling frightened from any potential menace. "I guess once the FBI came in, though, I should've taken it more seriously."

By the time promotion for *WrestleMania VII* began, Sgt. Slaughter had become one of the most reviled WWE Champions in history. His anti-American venom rivaled that of the Iron Sheik's nearly ten years earlier. Ironically, the same man who took down the Sheik was also charged with toppling Slaughter at *WrestleMania VII*: Hulk Hogan.

As *WrestleMania* drew closer, Slaughter began to attack the Hulkster with his unique brand of psychological warfare. One of his most effective stunts saw the champ send a Hogan T-shirt up in flames.

"The original plan was for me to burn the flag, but even I didn't think that was a good idea," admits Slaughter. "So I decided to burn the shirt, and I think it got the job done more than if I went in the other direction."

With patriotism at an all-time high, WWE chose the massive Los Angeles Memorial Coliseum to host *WrestleMania*. There were so many anti-Slaughter fans at the time that WWE didn't think twice about filling the place, despite urban legends to the contrary. Unfortunately, however, the Coliseum never wound up hosting the event.

"That's the most difficult part for me to accept," says Slaughter. "We were going to have 104,000 fans in there. Vince showed me the layout. He was going to have huge screens on each end of the football field. This was going to be the attendance record breaker. Then we got word that the Coliseum had so many threats against my life, and bomb threats as well, that Vince was going to have to secure the whole building, which was going to cost upwards of $4 million. So instead, we went inside the arena."

Although disappointed by the change in venue, Slaughter would take his title defense to the confines of the Los Angeles Memorial Sports Arena, which was decked out in red, white, and blue for the event. Uncharacteristically, Slaughter came out first for the match, followed by a flag-waving Hulk Hogan, who was greeted with a rousing patriotic ovation. The challenger used this support to carry him through much of the match. In the end, Hogan dropped the champ with a big boot before landing his lethal legdrop and picking up his unprecedented third WWE Championship.

As the capacity crowd hailed their hero, announcer Gorilla Monsoon proclaimed, "The war is now over!" He couldn't have been more wrong. After the event, Slaughter sought out Hogan in the locker-room area. While the unsuspecting Hulkster was celebrating his victory, the former champ tossed a fireball directly into his eyes. The disgusting act set up a series of rematches, but Slaughter was unable to regain the gold.

After his rivalry with Hogan, Slaughter struggled with which direction he should take his career. He hoped he could continue chasing the title as the Iraqi sympathizer. But when the Gulf War began, he backed off because people were dying in real-life situations.

"So I went out and asked for my country back," remembers Slaughter. "We did a series of vignettes at all different monuments and areas of historical interest. Finally, I went out and sang 'God Bless America,' and people were standing and cheering and holding up lighters. They accepted me back. When I got back through the curtain, Vince told me it was one of the most incredible things he'd ever seen. Later that night, I was teamed with 'Hacksaw' Jim Duggan. He was more of a patriot than Hogan. I thought about doing a double cross, but then decided it was better not to."

11

THE REAL WORLD CHAMPION

Hulk Hogan disposed of Sgt. Slaughter once and for all in August 1991. Around the same time, the legendary Ric Flair was engaged in a bitter battle with his WCW boss, Jim Herd.

"I hated working there," Flair recalls nearly two decades later. "Herd was not living up to his word with me. He was a very difficult guy. Plus he had no wrestling knowledge at all. Ted [Turner] was famous for hiring guys to patch holes in his company. It was like that with his baseball team too. The Atlanta Braves struggled for years until they brought Bobby Cox in to manage. He was a real baseball coach and the reason for their success."

Prior to being tapped as WCW's executive vice president, Herd was working as a station manager at KPLR-TV in St. Louis, Missouri. He also served as a regional manager for Pizza Hut. Neither job gave Herd the training necessary to run a wrestling company, and it showed in his questionable matchmaking. It wasn't long before Herd's shoddy wrestling IQ caused his stars to look at him quizzically, including Stan Hansen and Road Warrior Animal, who ultimately left WCW because of Herd's inability to grasp the business. Nobody in WCW, however, disliked Herd more than the Nature Boy.

Flair's contract expired during the summer of 1991, but he continued to compete as WCW Champion while negotiating a new deal. At one point during the negotiations, Herd called Flair while he was on vacation in Daytona Beach and told him to get on a flight to Baltimore so he could defend the title against Lex Luger. Fearing his negotiating leverage would be significantly lessened if he were to lose to Luger, Flair refused, telling Herd he wasn't going anywhere without a contract first.

Flair recalls an angered Herd screaming into the phone, "Do what I tell you or you will never wrestle again!" The Nature Boy laughed the threat off before ultimately suggesting he defend the title against Barry Windham instead, but not without a contract first. Again, Herd refused to grant Flair his wish.

After hanging up the phone, Flair began experiencing great amounts of guilt. He started to feel like he was letting his friends down, as well as the company he had worked for since 1974. So he called Herd to tell him he had changed his mind—he *would* compete against Windham without a contract.

"It's too late, screw it!" Herd told him. "I'm sending [head of security] Doug Dillinger to your house to come get the belt."

"Well, if he's coming to get the belt, make sure he has a check for $36,000 on him, because that's what you owe me. Otherwise, stick it up your ass," Flair responded, referring to the $25,000 deposit WCW Champions were required to give to prevent them from leaving the company with the title. Plus, Flair wanted an additional $11,000 in interest.

"You don't understand. Doug will be at your house to get the belt."

"Let me explain something to you," Flair countered. "Doug has been my friend for more than thirty years. I'll greet him at the door and shake his hand. But once he asks for the belt, I'll tell him to go screw himself. And then Doug will say, 'I understand, no problem,' before turning around and going back to work."

The contentious conversation with Herd effectively ended Flair's WCW tenure. But his career was far from over.

"As soon as I hung up the phone, I had a quiet talk with myself," remembers Flair. "I said: 'It's now or never, Ric.' So I called Vince. He didn't believe me, though. He said, 'Oh, God. I've heard this story before. Are you really going to come?' I told him that I was and I wouldn't be alone—I was bringing the WCW Championship with me."

Later that day, Flair stuffed his WCW title into a FedEx box and overnighted it to McMahon. Soon after, Bobby Heenan began showing up on WWE television with the WCW title, claiming the "real" world champion was on his way. He never mentioned Flair by name, but once everybody saw the gigantic WCW Championship, they knew it couldn't be anyone else.

Flair made his highly anticipated WWE debut in September 1991. Without hesitation, he targeted WWE Champion Hulk Hogan. "That belt that belongs to Hulk Hogan, as far as I'm concerned and the world's concerned, is cheap," said Flair during his initial WWE appearance. "It's an imitation of the real thing. Sure Hogan, you're the World Wrestling Federation Champion, but you're not the *real* world champion. You're not Ric Flair. Comparing what you own, the belt you have and the title you have, is like comparing prime rib to lunch meat."

The first verbal barb in the historic Flair-Hogan rivalry had been tossed. For nearly a decade, fans had drooled over the thought of the two biggest names in sports-entertainment finally squaring off. Before the monumental dream match could occur, however, Hogan had some unfinished business to take care of with the undefeated Undertaker. With only one year of WWE service to his credit the Deadman was still considered a relative newcomer, but he had already shown great promise, highlighted by a dominating performance over Jimmy Snuka at *WrestleMania VII*.

"THE THANKSGIVING TRADITION"

SURVIVOR SERIES®

THE GRAVEST CHALLENGE

CHAMPIONSHIP MATCH

MAIN EVENT

VS

CHALLENGE

**CHAMPION
HULK HOGAN™**

**THE UNDERTAKER™
MANAGED BY PAUL BEARER™**

ALSO FEATURING
SUPERSTAR TAG TEAM ELIMINATION MATCHES

New Night!

**THANKSGIVING EVE,
WEDNESDAY, NOVEMBER 27**

8PM EASTERN/5PM PACIFIC
REPLAY AT 11PM EASTERN/8PM PACIFIC

The Hulkster and Undertaker battled at the 1991 *Survivor Series* in a match that was dubbed Hogan's "Gravest Challenge." Most fans assumed the champ would somehow find a way to topple his massive challenger, just as he had done to his competition so many times before. But those fans failed to account for Flair. With the referee's attention diverted, the Nature Boy slipped a chair into the ring. Undertaker then scooped up Hogan and delivered a skull-crushing Tombstone directly on top of the chair. With a look of satisfaction proudly displayed on his face, Flair sauntered back to the locker room as the referee made the three count. Hogan had shockingly lost the WWE Championship to Undertaker, thanks in large part to the interference of Ric Flair.

The impact of the Tombstone resulted in a several-day hospital stay for the Hulkster. His team of doctors advised him to have surgery to fuse together the disks in his neck. Hogan, however, wanted none of that. Surgery would require a lengthy stay on the sidelines, which meant he would not be able to seek revenge from Undertaker. So despite having little feeling in his arms, Hogan checked out of the hospital and prepared for his rematch.

Immediately following the "Gravest Challenge," backstage interviewer Gene Okerlund tracked down WWE President Jack Tunney to demand the controversial situation be cleared.

"The referee's decision is final and cannot be challenged by me," said Tunney, while a visibly angered Okerlund fought to maintain his composure. "However, it is well within my authority to order a rematch at the earliest possible date. Therefore, it is my decision that Undertaker meet Hulk Hogan in a rematch for the [WWE] title this Tuesday in Texas [December 3, 1991, on Pay-Per-View]. And furthermore, I will physically be at ringside to ensure a fair and just outcome."

Tunney's announcement of a rematch shook the wrestling world to its foundation. Never before had WWE produced two Pay-Per-View events within one week of each other. The controversy surrounding Undertaker's win, however, deemed it necessary. The event was appropriately called *This Tuesday in Texas,* and it was Hulk Hogan's chance to right the wrong done by Ric Flair.

Like *Survivor Series,* the rematch was marred by the Nature Boy's meddling. But before a repeat performance could completely unfold, Hogan managed to neutralize Flair with a steel chair to the back. The force of the blow caused the Nature Boy to fall forward, directly on top of Tunney.

With the WWE President out cold at ringside, Hogan was able to wrest Undertaker manager Paul Bearer's mystical urn away. He popped off the top and poured some poor soul's ashes onto the ring mat. He then grabbed a handful of ashes and tossed them directly into Undertaker's eyes, temporarily blinding the champ long enough for Hogan to roll him up for the win.

A mere six days after losing to Undertaker at *Survivor Series,* Hogan defeated the Deadman at *This Tuesday in Texas* to claim his unprecedented fourth WWE Championship.

The celebration, however, did not last long.

The route Hulk Hogan took to regain the gold was highly controversial, and as a result, the status of his reign was in great question. The following weekend, Tunney appeared on WWE television via satellite from his office at the company's headquarters: "As president of World Wrestling Federation, I am fully aware that the decisions of this office are not always popular, and that this one will be no exception. However, I cannot stand idly by and take little action in the face of such grievous circumstances. This past Tuesday in Texas, during the Undertaker–Hulk Hogan Championship Match, I witnessed with my own eyes what I believe was a flagrant and far-reaching oversight on the part of the referee. Now, the referee's decision is final. I will not challenge his official decision. However, under these circumstances, I have little choice but to decree the [WWE] title vacant."

Tunney scheduled the vacancy to be filled at the following month's *Royal Rumble,* where the winner of the thirty-man, over-the-top-rope Rumble Match would be declared the new champion. With so much at stake, the event was easily the most anticipated *Royal Rumble* in the five-year history of the event. All the big names took part, including Sid Justice, Randy Savage, Roddy Piper, Ted DiBiase, a young Shawn Michaels, and Ric Flair. The two most recent WWE Champions, Undertaker and Hogan, would also compete in the match. Recognizing their recent history with the title, Tunney gave them a slight edge over the competition by ensuring their draw would be no lower than twenty.

The late draw failed to help Undertaker, who was eliminated by Hogan after approximately fourteen minutes of action. The Hulkster, on the other

Undertaker clotheslines Hulk Hogan.

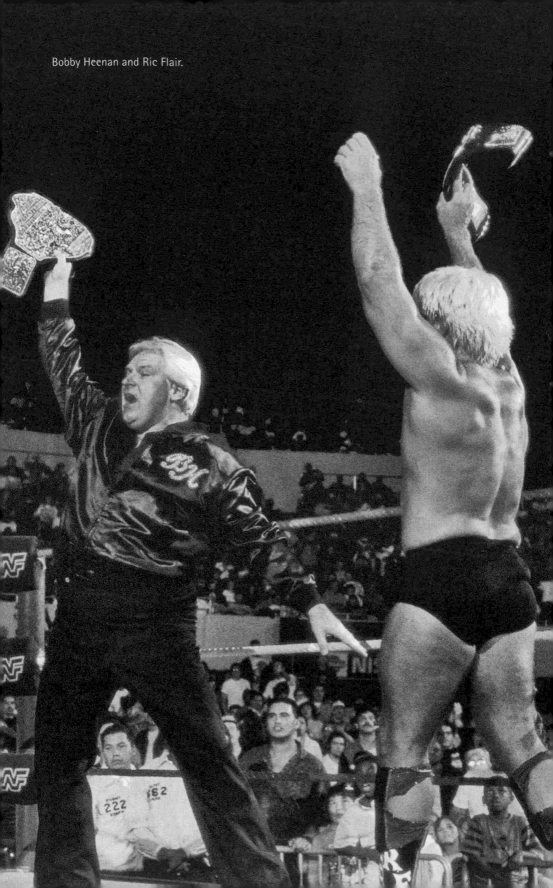

Bobby Heenan and Ric Flair.

hand, looked primed to take the prize after entering in the twenty-sixth spot. But Sid Justice had other plans. The chiseled Superstar snuck behind the unsuspecting Hogan and dumped him over the top rope, thus crushing his hopes of becoming a five-time WWE Champion. Irate, Hogan screamed at Justice from the floor before grabbing his hand and trying to pull him over the top rope. While this was going on, Ric Flair quickly slipped behind Justice and tossed him over the top to win the Rumble Match and fill the six-week-long WWE Championship vacancy.

Ric Flair's victory shocked everybody in attendance. Of course, they recognized that he was one of the greatest to ever compete, but he had entered the Rumble with the third draw, meaning he was in the ring battling for a full grueling hour. Prior to Flair's victory, the longest a Rumble winner had ever competed was Hogan's twenty-minute appearance in 1991.

After the Rumble Match, Flair made his way to the locker-room area, where Tunney formally presented him with the WWE Championship. With a tear in his eye, Ric Flair proclaimed that winning the title was the greatest moment of his life. Nearly two decades later, the Nature Boy still feels the same way.

"That was the biggest moment of my career, which is saying a lot. It meant so much to regain that championship status, especially since I was representing WWE, which was a much bigger company than where I had been. It was a huge night. I was completely overwhelmed."

12

A FLAIR FOR
THE GOLD

Ric Flair's victory at the *Royal Rumble* made him only the second man in history to capture both the NWA and WWE Championships. The other was the original Nature Boy, Buddy Rogers, with whom Flair shared so many similarities beyond their nickname. Not only were both Superstars champions in NWA and WWE, but both also sported bright blond hair, bronzed skin, and an affinity for the figure-four leglock. Additionally, Flair and Rogers were both known for their amazing endurance in the ring. Neither Nature Boy was afraid of competing for sixty minutes.

"At the time I became WWE Champion, WWE main events usually lasted ten minutes," recalls Flair. "But it took me twenty minutes just to warm up. I had to feel the way the crowd was responding. I'm used to psychology, feeling the crowd, giving them what they paid to see. I'm not saying nobody else did that, but I just had a hard time wrestling a twenty-minute world championship match. I liked to build the intrigue and suspense."

With each passing day of Flair's WWE Championship reign, fans and colleagues began to recognize and appreciate the unique style he brought to the title. That admiration helped the Nature Boy finally rid himself of the WCW negativity that was still haunting him.

"During that reign, I began to feel whole about myself again. I re-established all my self-confidence. WCW struggled to find a role for me, and they were always trying to replace me. Then three months later, I was the champion of the flagship wrestling company. So that was huge for me; plus, it was so much fun. Being champion just made the party even bigger. When I was champion, I never had a hard time getting a drink. Ironically, the truth is that the champ should be the one buying the drinks—that's always been the case. Years later, when David Arquette won the WCW Championship, I made him leave the hotel bar to go up to his room and get the belt and his credit card. I said, 'Champ, you're buying this whole damn hotel drinks all night long.' And he did."

Partying like a champion is part of the job, according to Flair, who later pulled the same "Arquette tactic" on John Cena when he won the WWE Championship and Santino Marella after capturing the Intercontinental title in Milan, Italy.

One person who did whimper after partying hard with Flair was his manager Bobby Heenan. After traveling with the champ for three days, an exhausted Heenan turned to Flair on the plane and said, "I hate you, I hate you, I hate you! I hope your hair falls out and comes back red. When we land in New York, I'm telling Vince I'm done with you!"

Luckily, Heenan was only partially serious, and the two continued their amazing working relationship.

On February 1, 1992, Heenan and Executive Consultant Mr. Perfect stood by Flair's side at a press conference to announce the Nature Boy's *WrestleMania VIII* opponent. Among the possible challengers present at the press conference were Undertaker, Roddy Piper, Hulk Hogan, Randy Savage, and Sid Justice. According to WWE President Jack Tunney, the decision to name a number-one contender was especially difficult, but after careful consideration, as well as examining the public's demand, he ultimately awarded the WWE Championship opportunity to the Hulkster. Finally, sports-entertainment fans were going to get the dream match they longed for: Hulk Hogan versus Ric Flair at *WrestleMania*.

Sid took the snub the hardest, calling Tunney's decision bogus before tossing several verbal barbs in Hogan's direction. Over the next few weeks—sans a brief friendship—the tension between Sid and Hogan escalated to monumental levels. WWE officials had a difficult situation on their hands. The Hulkster was scheduled to face Flair at *WrestleMania*, but Hogan's war with Sid was coming to a head quickly. It was ultimately decided that a battle between Hogan and Sid could not wait until after *WrestleMania*. As a result, Hogan was pulled from his match with Flair and put into a contest with Sid. It was later announced that Savage would fill the void in the WWE Championship Match against Flair.

To this day, WWE fans still talk about what could've been at *WrestleMania VIII*. Many believe the wrong decision was made when Hogan was pulled out of the match with the Nature Boy. Flair, however, looks at it a bit differently.

"I don't regret it at all. I don't look back at stuff like that. I never asked for an explanation and never heard one. But I wasn't disappointed at all. I got to walk out the door in Indianapolis at *WrestleMania VIII* and wrestle Randy Savage. Hogan was wrestling Sid. You tell me who was in a better spot."

Heading into *WrestleMania VIII*, Flair began an intense campaign of mind games designed to force Randy Savage into questioning his relationship with his wife, Elizabeth. While showing an enlarged photo of a swimsuit-clad Elizabeth and the Nature Boy canoodling by a hot tub, Flair claimed that the beautiful brunette was his property well before Savage ever came along. The champ went so far as to tell the notoriously jealous Savage that his wife thought of the Nature Boy as the world's greatest wrestler, as well as the world's greatest lover.

Saving the best for last, Flair told Savage that he had an even more provocative photo of his wife that he was going to display for the world to see at *WrestleMania*. The embarrassment and humiliation was too much for Elizabeth to handle. In the weeks leading up to *WrestleMania,* she became visibly distraught, while the rage continued to build inside the Macho Man. When Savage's name was finally announced on April 5, 1992, the challenger bolted down the aisle as if he were shot out of a cannon. Less than twenty minutes later, the Macho Man gained the vengeance he was after when he defeated Flair with a roll-up from behind.

Elizabeth jumped into the ring to celebrate with her husband. As she tended to her battered man, a defeated Flair grabbed her and kissed her on the lips. In a rare moment of rage, Elizabeth slapped the Nature Boy across the face, followed by another slap, and another. Just as Savage had done early on in the match, she was releasing weeks of pent-up anger on Flair.

Savage and Elizabeth were later vindicated when *WWE Magazine* revealed that Flair had doctored the photos. The real pictures showed the loving couple sharing private moments; Flair had simply superimposed himself in the Macho Man's place.

Following *WrestleMania,* Randy Savage and Elizabeth believed they were finally free from Flair's scheming, finally able to close the book on a pain-

One of the controversial doctored photos of Ric Flair and Elizabeth.

ful chapter in their relationship. Furthermore, the WWE Championship Committee had selected Ultimate Warrior as the Macho Man's *SummerSlam* opponent, meaning Flair was out of the picture both personally and professionally. Or so they thought.

When Flair learned that Warrior was getting the title opportunity at *SummerSlam* instead of him, he launched another series of well-calculated mind games. This time, his psychological manipulation left both Savage and Warrior believing the other had joined forces with Mr. Perfect. In reality, neither man was in cahoots with Flair's executive consultant—it was all just an excuse for Flair and Mr. Perfect to get close to the ring at *SummerSlam*, where they would wind up brutally attacking Savage's leg with a chair.

The pain caused by steel meeting bone forced Randy Savage to curl up into a fetal position while the referee started to count. Valiantly, the Macho Man tried to recover, but the pain was too great. The ref had no choice but to count Savage out. As a result, Warrior was declared the winner. He was not, however, awarded the WWE Championship because the title cannot change hands on a count-out.

Nobody could ever accuse Randy Savage of not being a fighting champion. In the days following *SummerSlam*, he agreed to defend his gold against

One of the real photos, with Randy Savage and Elizabeth.

Flair, despite not being able to put any weight on his left leg. This unbridled display of machismo ultimately led to Savage's final moments as champion.

Following some outside interference by newcomer Razor Ramon, Flair was able to cinch in his figure-four leglock. Savage refused to give in to the torturous hold, as the capacity crowd marveled at the champ's courage to continue. Finally, though, the pain had become too much for Savage's body to withstand. He slowly drifted out of consciousness as the referee counted his shoulders down for the three count.

As Ric Flair celebrated his second WWE Championship victory, Randy Savage lay unconscious on the mat, not even realizing his reign had ended. His WWE career never fully rebounded from the loss. He would go on to briefly battle Razor Ramon before settling into his role as color commentator, as well as an instantly recognizable voiceover and character actor.

Ric Flair and Mr. Perfect celebrate the defeat of Randy Savage.

13

THE EXCELLENCE
OF EXECUTION

With the WWE Championship back around his waist, Ric Flair

had visions of a very lengthy reign. One month in, however, a

freak injury jeopardized those hopes.

"I was wrestling Ultimate Warrior in Phoenix in October

1992," remembers Flair. "Out of nowhere, Warrior dropped me

on my head. After a while, I finally got up but I quickly fell back down again. Then I got up and I fell down, over and over. I had no idea what was going on. Turns out I was diagnosed with an inner-ear condition that caused me to lose my bearings. I just couldn't work anymore."

Despite barely being able to balance himself, Flair agreed to defend his title against Bret "Hit Man" Hart in Saskatoon, Canada, on October 12, 1992. At the time, Hart was considered a "young veteran," having competed professionally for sixteen years (eight with WWE). Over this time, he had compiled an impressive résumé, consisting of two World Tag Team Championships and two Intercontinental Championships. But this was his first true crack at immortality. Ironically, the opportunity took place in a town with which he was quite familiar.

"I had my very first match in Saskatoon," Bret Hart admits nearly eighteen years later. "I didn't have much of a physique in those days. I remember walking out to face Flair for my title shot and thinking to myself, 'This is where it all started.' It was special to come back and compete in Saskatoon of all places, especially because it was one of my dad's towns."

The Hit Man's father was legendary trainer Stu Hart. The elder Hart is credited with helping launch the careers of such greats as the Junkyard Dog, Japanese sensation Jushin Liger, "Superstar" Billy Graham, and the British Bulldog, among others. Hart's wrestling promotion, Stampede Wrestling, also ran shows throughout much of Canada, including Saskatoon. This time around, however, Saskatoon was WWE country, more specifically Bret Hart country. Utilizing his patented Sharpshooter, the "Excellence of Execution" was able to force Flair into submission and finally realize his dream of becoming WWE Champion.

Hart's wife, two eldest children, father, and brother Bruce were all in attendance that night. But none of them got to share in the joy with the new titleholder. "I had two really bad injuries. I dislocated my finger and rolled my ankle. I actually thought I broke my finger; it was bent sideways. It was shaped like an L. So I celebrated my victory with a trip to the hospital. I was there until about 1:30 A.M. Then I went back to my hotel room and tried to get some sleep."

Bret Hart's victory over Ric Flair ushered in a new generation of sports-entertainment. Unlike Hulk Hogan, Hart weighed in at a relatively

Bret Hart vs. Ric Flair.

light 235 pounds—he didn't have muscles on top of muscles like the champions before him. Instead, the toned-down Superstar used his superior technical wrestling ability to wow fans. This new formula for success ultimately proved its worth, but not before some initial growing pains.

"I realized that wrestling was going through a transition," admits Hart. "Hogan was such a big entity, and in a lot of ways I had to fill Hogan's shoes. But he was more of a cartoon character from a wrestling standpoint. He was such a phenomenon that, by the time Hulkamania had played out, I found myself as the champion. That's when the business took a sharp turn. It stopped being about cartoon characters, and it became more about the actual wrestling. I was the first champion who centered on the wrestling and title matches. As a result, the title suddenly meant something. When Hogan had it, everybody assumed there would be a happy ending every night. But with me as champion, there was a little more uncertainty. When I walked out, most fans thought maybe the title would change hands that night—it gave them more of a chance to be surprised at the results."

Survivor Series 1992 marked Hart's first major title defense. It was against Shawn Michaels—the same man who would help screw the Hit Man out of the WWE Championship five years later at the same event. The Hart-Michaels main event was a far cry from the two masses of humanity (Hogan and Undertaker) who had battled over the title just one year prior at *Survivor Series*. But what the Hit Man and HBK lacked in size, they more than made up for in technical ability.

At first, fans weren't sure what to expect out of Bret Hart versus Shawn Michaels. There was very little buildup to the match on television, which was very uncommon heading into a major Pay-Per-View, but fans kept an open mind.

Prior to the battle, interviewer "Mean" Gene Okerlund ran through the list of opponents Bret Hart had successfully defended his WWE Championship against. The Berzerker, Virgil, Papa Shango, The Mountie . . . and the list continued. Quantity surely could not be questioned. Quality, however, was a much different story. These Superstars were far from elite. So when then-Intercontinental Champion Michaels confidently strolled to the ring at *Survivor Series*, fans began to think Hart might be in some serious trouble, considering he had yet to defend the gold against a truly worthy competitor.

Once the bell rang, Bret Hart quickly put all the fans' doubts to rest. He went on the offensive early, utilizing a series of hammerlocks and headlocks—moves that were often foreign to WWE Championship Matches of the Hogan era. As the match progressed, so did the scientific wrestling, but at a considerably quicker rate. Sunset flips. Flying cross-bodies. Small packages. Russian leg sweeps. Hart and Michaels were executing lightning-fast moves. And the fans were eating it up. In the end, it was the Hit Man picking up the win with his signature Sharpshooter.

Bret Hart kissed his championship after the match, as Ohio's sold-out Richfield Coliseum showered him with praise. The victory not only solidified the Hit Man's reign as legitimate, it also turned WWE's fans on to a new brand of championship matches. Despite all the adulation, however, Hart was still trying to adjust to his new role of champion.

"It still hadn't sunk in. I couldn't believe it was happening, and I couldn't believe it was *me*. I began to feel a great sense of responsibility to everybody in the dressing room and the company because I felt it was important to be ready every night and be prepared to carry the torch and be the champion. I changed my lifestyle. I didn't go out and have beers with the other wrestlers anymore, mainly because I felt an obligation to be on the ball every night. I just changed my life. I kinda had to pinch myself every day."

The newly focused Bret Hart used his Sharpshooter once again to earn a Pay-Per-View victory, this time over Razor Ramon at the 1993 *Royal Rumble*. As Hart celebrated his victory in the back, undefeated newcomer Yokozuna was tossing Randy Savage over the top rope to win the Rumble Match. The 1993 Rumble marked the first time in history that the winner was granted a WWE Championship opportunity at *WrestleMania*. As a result of the new stipulation, the 500-pound monster was locked in for the main event at the biggest event of the year.

Caesars Palace played host to *WrestleMania IX*, the first-ever outdoor *WrestleMania*. In keeping with the Caesars Palace theme, the Pay-Per-View was dubbed the "World's Largest Toga Party," which required the announcers and television crew to wear togas. Ring announcer Howard Finkel even changed his name to Finkus Maximus for the event.

Considering Yokozuna's massive size, fans anticipated a very slow and plodding main event. But the contest turned out to be more technical than expected.

"Yoko was actually an amazing athlete and a very formidable opponent. I always had pretty good chemistry with him. I was able to bring out the best in him and vice versa. People forget how young he was; he was just a kid when he was working with me at *Wrestle-Mania IX*."

Despite Yokozuna's prowess, at *WrestleMania IX* he resorted to cheating to accomplish his goal. While Hart had Yokozuna's massive legs locked in the Sharpshooter, Mr. Fuji pulled out a bag of salt and tossed it into the champ's eyes. The underhanded tactic temporarily blinded Hart, long enough for Yokozuna to cover him for the win.

Six months after defeating Ric Flair in a technical classic to win the WWE Championship, Bret Hart had the title stolen from him by Yokozuna. The loss was especially tough to swallow, considering the Hit Man had spent those six months establishing the entertainment value of technical wrestling. Then, with one handful of salt, it was all gone.

"When I lost the belt to Yokozuna at *WrestleMania IX*, that was, believe it or not, the first time I realized I was the champion," claims Hart. "When I lost it, that was when I thought it was *my* belt and I should have it back. I started to appreciate my position as WWE Champion after I lost it. I didn't have the confidence yet during that first reign—I kept thinking I could lose it any day. But when it changed hands, I suddenly realized I was champion of the company . . . even when I didn't have the belt. For the rest of my run with WWE, it was always *my* belt. I was at my peak for the rest of my time there."

A defeated Hart slowly began to regain his sight as he made his way out of the ring at Caesars Palace. Hulk Hogan, who had competed in a Tag Team Match earlier in the evening, ran to ringside to help the Hit Man find his way to the back.

Then Mr. Fuji proceeded to make the most ill-advised managerial decision in the history of sports-entertainment.

"Hogan!" Fuji screamed. "We will put up the new [WWE] heavyweight belt in the ring right now!"

Hogan was reluctant at first, but eventually he accepted the challenge

after Hart gave his blessing. One clothesline and a legdrop later and the Hulkster was WWE Champion for an amazing fifth time. Even more astounding was the brevity of Yokozuna's reign. He only held the title for two minutes and seven seconds—only Andre the Giant held it for a shorter period of time.

Hogan's fifth WWE Championship reign came close to never happening. A few days prior to *WrestleMania IX*, the Hulkster went Jet Skiing with fellow WWE Superstar Brutus Beefcake and *Baywatch* stunt coordinator Ellis Edwards. During the excursion, Hogan was tossed from his Ski headfirst. When he brought his head back above water, he noticed another Ski coming right at him. His life jacket prevented him from ducking fully back under the water, and the Jet Ski collided with his face at forty miles per hour. The impact broke his orbital socket.

Hogan's doctor told him to not get on a plane, let alone compete at *WrestleMania IX*. He ignored him. Instead, the Hulk showed up at Caesars Palace with a huge black eye. When fans saw it, rumors began running rampant regarding the true cause of the injury: The most popular urban myth that still exists today claims Randy Savage knocked Hogan out after learning he had an affair with Elizabeth.

The fifth time around for Hulk Hogan proved to be much less memorable than his previous WWE Championship reigns. By this time, fans wanted more of the Bret Hart–style main event matches. Plus, Hogan's heart wasn't truly in it anymore. He was more focused on making it big in Hollywood. In his 2002 autobiography, *Hollywood Hulk Hogan*, he admitted to looking at his new reign as little more than a payday—obviously not the attitude WWE expected from its champion.

With a listless Hogan representing WWE as champ, business began to drop. Hart saw the decline in popularity as an opportunity to regain what he believed was rightfully his.

"I had a feeling that they would see that going with Hogan was a mistake and that I would get my chance to be champion again. I actually got the sense that I would be challenging Hogan at *SummerSlam* that year. And I figured I'd probably beat him. But that never happened because Hogan was uncomfortable getting in the ring with me, even though he said he would be happy to do it to my face."

Hulk Hogan vs. Yokozuna.

Regardless, Hulk Hogan never made it to *SummerSlam*. While defending the title against Yokozuna in June at the *King of the Ring*, the Hulkster was victimized by a mysterious cameraman who climbed the ring apron and shot a fireball into the champ's face. The evil act blinded Hogan long enough for Yokozuna to land his big legdrop to pick up the win and the WWE Championship.

14

BANZAI

Yokozuna's second reign proved much more successful than his first. As the days passed, he continued to do everything he could to ensure he would be a success, including packing on an unhealthy amount of weight. By July 4, 1993, his colossal frame had grown to an immovable 568 pounds.

To prove it, Yokozuna hosted an Independence Day Stars and Stripes Challenge aboard the U.S.S. *Intrepid*. The event was open to any American athlete who believed he could slam the mighty Yokozuna. In the unlikely event the champ was bodyslammed, the winner would receive a free Chevrolet Silverado.

Athletes from all over the world showed up to the challenge. Representing the National Football League were Lee Rouson of the New York Giants and Bill Fralic of the Detroit Lions; the Pittsburgh Penguins' Peter Taglianetti stood in for the National Hockey League; and Scott Burrell of the Charlotte Hornets represented the National Basketball Association. All sported superb résumés, but none were able to lift Yokozuna.

Many of WWE's best even attempted to slam the champ. Scott Steiner, Bob Backlund, Tatanka, and Randy Savage gave it a try, but all failed. Crush came the closest, but he was only able to get Yokozuna a few inches off the ground.

As Mr. Fuji and Yokozuna celebrated their apparent victory, thunderous sounds began to fall from the sky. The thousands of fans aboard the *Intrepid* looked up to find a helicopter coming in for a landing. A

Luger vs. Yokozuna.

collective "who is it?" rang out from the crowd, as they all wanted to know which Superstar was brave enough to stand up to Yokozuna, especially after so many great names had just failed in their attempts to slam the big man. Their hero exited the helicopter in the unlikely form of Lex Luger.

Luger was far from popular at the time. Introduced to the fans earlier in the year as "The Narcissist" by manager Bobby Heenan, Luger displayed an air of arrogance that made him impossible to like. But on this day, something was very different. His red, white, and blue shirt offered a sign that he cared more about defending his country's honor than his own personal goals. Additionally, he forcefully tossed the hated Heenan into the Chevrolet Silverado while on his way to the ring. This was all the fans needed.

"Lex! Lex! Lex!" shouted the crowd, as Luger stepped into the ring. They could sense they were about to witness something truly historic, and Luger didn't disappoint. He whacked Yokozuna with his forearm, which was surgically packed with a six-inch steel plate following a motorcycle accident. The force of the forearm blast wobbled the big man. Luger then hoisted the gigantic Superstar up and over. He had succeeded in doing the unthinkable: Lex Luger had bodyslammed Yokozuna.

The "Bodyslam Heard Around the World" made Luger an instant fan favorite and positioned him for a WWE Championship Match at *Summer-Slam* 1993. He spent the next several weeks riding his tour bus, the Lex Express, from coast to coast greeting the great American fans. Thousands of people showed up in each town, hoping they could get a glimpse of their new hero. All of them offered words of encouragement and told Luger to bring the title back home to America.

SummerSlam was held that year in Michigan's Palace of Auburn Hills. The card featured several high-profile matches, including Shawn Michaels versus Mr. Perfect for the Intercontinental Championship, and Undertaker versus Giant Gonzalez in a Rest in Peace Match. While each of the undercard matches certainly delivered, there was an excitement floating through the arena akin to what a young kid on Christmas Eve feels. The fans just wanted to get to the main event.

Nine matches later, they finally got their wish. Yokozuna and Luger kicked off the contest with an extended stare down before Mr. Fuji attempted to run into the ring and attack the challenger from behind. Right off the bat, it was clear that Luger was going to need eyes in the back of his head if he wanted to be successful.

The fans in attendance tried to even the odds with their vocal support. "USA! USA! USA!" reverberated throughout the arena as Luger lifted the mighty Yokozuna and slammed him to the mat, just as he did on the hallowed deck of the U.S.S. *Intrepid* on America's birthday. As the champion climbed to his feet, Luger charged at full force, nailing Yokozuna with his steel-plated forearm. The impact sent the big man barreling to the arena floor. With the champ on the outside, the referee counted to ten and awarded the match to Luger via count-out.

Unfortunately for Luger, he could not win the title on a count-out, meaning that, despite the loss, Yokozuna was still the champion. Luger didn't let that get in the way of his good time, though. Alongside the Steiner Brothers, Tatanka, and Randy Savage, he celebrated as if he had just won the WWE Championship. Red, white, and blue balloons fell from the arena ceiling, while Luger proudly waved the American flag. The fans, on the other hand, were not as joyous. They saw the count-out victory as a major disappointment. To them, anything less than bringing the title back to America was considered a failure, especially after investing so much emotion into the match. As a result, Luger lost a great deal of his momentum after *SummerSlam*, even though he had technically won.

Yokozuna and Luger crossed paths once again in November 1993, when each captained a team at *Survivor Series*. Luger proved to be the sole survivor of the match, but once again, his win failed to advance his career. Instead, most of the night's focus revolved around Yokozuna's inability to inflict damage to Undertaker, despite hitting him with a Banzai Drop and slamming his head into the steel ring steps. For the first time ever, fear began to show itself on the champ's face as he realized there was nothing he could do to injure the Deadman.

The confrontation between Yokozuna and Undertaker resulted in a WWE Championship Match at the 1994 *Royal Rumble*. In the weeks leading up to the match, the champ's American Spokesperson, Jim Cornette, used a little of his Smokey Mountain magic to sneak some fine print into the contract, stating that the *Royal Rumble* would be the Deadman's one-and-only opportunity at Yokozuna's title. The Phenom's manager, Paul Bearer, fired back with a stipulation of his own, which turned the contest into a Casket Match.

The rules of the contest heavily favored Undertaker. He had already proved he could defeat a big man in this type of match when he beat Kamala at the 1992 *Survivor Series*. Furthering his advantage was Yokozuna's intense phobia of caskets. Even saying the word out loud sent the champ into a nervous panic.

The combination of Yokozuna's inability to inflict damage to Undertaker, coupled with the champ's fear of caskets, left Mr. Fuji searching for a Plan B. While studying the rules of the match, which included no disqualification and no count-out, the devious manager found a loophole. Instead of asking his man to beat down Undertaker, he would take advantage of the loose rules and hire a group of thugs to do the dirty work for him.

At first, Undertaker was able to fend off Fuji's henchmen, including the Great Kabuki, Crush, Genichiro Tenryu, and Bam Bam Bigelow. But when the gang grew to include Jeff Jarrett, the Headshrinkers, Adam Bomb, and Diesel, Undertaker's luck had run out. It wasn't long before they were able to stuff the Deadman into the coffin and lock the lid, signifying the end of the match.

Yokozuna held his title high, as his hired henchmen pushed the casket containing the Phenom toward the back. Thoughts of an Undertaker-less WWE began to sink into the minds of the stunned Providence Civic Center crowd. Was this truly the demise of the Deadman? It certainly appeared so.

But then, out of nowhere, Undertaker's signature gong sounded throughout the arena. A mysterious smoke spilled from the casket as the building turned pitch-black. In a moment that can only be explained as supernatural, Undertaker, who was still in the casket, somehow appeared on the arena's big screen.

"Be not proud," he said in a gravelly voice. "The spirit of Undertaker lives within the soul of all mankind. The eternal flame of life that cannot be extinguished. The origin of which cannot be explained. The answer lives in the everlasting spirit. Soon all mankind will witness the rebirth of Undertaker. I will not rest in peace."

In one of the most memorable moments in WWE history, the Deadman then levitated from the screen all the way up to the arena ceiling. It was the last anybody saw of Undertaker for eight long months.

• • •

The site of the Phenom floating to the ceiling certainly was a tough act to follow, but once the smoke finally cleared, the first two participants in the annual *Royal Rumble* Match made their way to the ring to give it their best shot. On the line was the prestigious spot in *WrestleMania*'s main event against WWE Champion Yokozuna.

After nearly one hour of action, Bret Hart and Lex Luger proved to be the final two men standing. They feverishly exchanged right hands as they backed into the ropes. Hart then applied pressure against Luger's body, sending both men over the top rope at the same exact time. To the naked eye, the result appeared to be a tie. Replays also proved inconclusive, as the referees argued over who the true winner was. After several minutes of heated discussion among the officials, Howard Finkel finally grabbed his microphone.

"Ladies and gentleman, the winner of the 1994 [WWE] *Royal Rumble . . .*" Luger's music began to play throughout the arena, as his supporters in attendance cheered.

Referee Earl Hebner stopped Finkel before he could announce Luger's name. According to Hebner, Hart was the real winner. So Finkel grabbed his microphone once again.

"Ladies and gentlemen, the winner of the 1994 [WWE] *Royal Rumble . . .*" This time it was Hart's music playing loudly throughout the arena, while his supporters cheered wildly. Judging from the crowd reaction, it was evident the Hit Man had considerably more fans in attendance.

Finally, WWE President Jack Tunney made his way to the ring to clear up the controversy. After three minutes of conversation with the referees, he made his all-important decision and relayed it to Finkel.

"Ladies and gentlemen, the winner of the 1994 [WWE] *Royal Rumble . . .*" A look of confusion overtook the ring announcer's face, and he walked back over to Tunney to whisper, "Are you sure?"

Tunney was sure.

"Ladies and gentlemen," continued Finkel. "The winner of the 1994 [WWE] *Royal Rumble . . .*" He paused. "The *winners* are Lex Luger and Bret 'Hit Man' Hart."

After more than six minutes of confusion and consultation, Finkel's final announcement did little to clear up the *WrestleMania X* WWE Championship picture. With two winners, fans were still left wondering which Superstar would go on to face Yokozuna. If it were up to the crowd reaction, however, it would've been Hart.

"A lot of times, it came down to a popularity contest between me and Lex," claims Hart more than fifteen years later. "When I put my hands up, the whole crowd roared for me. When Lex did the same, there was a roar, but it wasn't the same. But I think Lex was a little misunderstood. He wasn't very personable with the fans. And he openly admitted that he didn't really like to talk with fans or have them come up and ask for autographs. But he was a great guy. He would give you the shirt off his back. From a work standpoint, though, I don't know that we were in the same league."

After several days of carefully considering his options, Tunney finally ruled that both Superstars would get an opportunity for the gold at *WrestleMania X*, starting with Luger, who was awarded first crack after winning a ceremonial coin toss. Luger's victory in the toss also meant that Hart's title opportunity would only come after he battled his younger brother Owen Hart, in the opening match of *WrestleMania*. After spending nearly all of their childhoods competing against each other in their father's famed Dungeon, it was no surprise that the brothers' battle was an instant classic.

"Owen and I knew each other's styles so well," recalls Bret. "It never seemed like hard work with him. You could wake us up at 4:00 A.M. and we could have a great match. I had the same thing with Curt Hennig. He was one of the best wrestlers in the world. Owen was the same: a total pro every night."

On the night of *WrestleMania X,* not only was Owen a total pro, he was also the better man. When a Hit Man victory roll went awry, the crafty Owen was able to drop his knees over his brother's shoulders to pick up the win. The victory served two purposes for Owen. First, it helped him finally jump from the shadow of his successful brother. Second, he damaged Bret's oft-injured leg enough to put his upcoming WWE Championship Match in serious jeopardy.

Prior to the Luger-Yokozuna WWE Championship Match, Mr. Perfect was announced as the bout's special guest referee. The assignment seemingly favored Luger, who was also a heavy fan favorite heading into the contest.

Bret Hart celebrates with Lex Luger and Razor Ramon.

In the end, however, putting Perfect in the referee stripes proved costly for the challenger.

Just when it looked like Lex Luger had Yokozuna where he wanted him, Mr. Fuji and Cornette climbed to the ring apron to distract the challenger. Instead of going for the pin, Luger took their bait and forcefully pulled both men into the ring before finally going for the cover on Yokozuna. Mr. Perfect, however, refused to count. Instead, he tended to the fallen Cornette and Mr. Fuji. This puzzled Luger, who was beginning to feel his championship hopes slip away. In an attempt to expedite the three count, Luger gave the special guest referee the slightest shove, as if to say, "Hurry up, make the count." Mr. Perfect did not appreciate the act of physicality and surprisingly disqualified Luger on the spot.

Yokozuna's disqualification victory over Luger set up a rematch with his *WrestleMania IX* opponent, Bret Hart. The legendary Roddy Piper served as the referee, and despite having a rollercoaster relationship with the Hit Man over the years, he called the action down the middle. In fact, when Cornette tried to climb the ring apron, Piper knocked the American spokesperson right off—a far cry from Mr. Perfect's questionable officiating style. In the end, Yokozuna fell to the mat after losing his balance while attempting a Banzai Drop. This allowed Hart to slide in for the pin and the win.

Hart had ended Yokozuna's ten-month reign as WWE Champion, but more important for him, he had finally erased his *WrestleMania IX* loss to the big man. After the match, the majority of the locker room, including Randy Savage and Lex Luger, spilled out into the ring to celebrate with the Hit Man. They hoisted him up on their shoulders as the sold-out Madison Square Garden crowd showed their appreciation for the new champ.

"I always had a lot of respect for Randy Savage. To have him in the ring with me meant a lot. And Lex Luger too. He was always very gracious about the entire situation. He came up to me after *WrestleMania X* and told me that I deserved to be the champion. He fully supported my championship reign—I never forgot that, because that's rare."

15

A FAMILY AFFAIR

Dripping with perspiration—both his own and Yokozuna's—

Bret Hart finally made his way to the Madison Square Garden

locker-room area to commence celebrating his second WWE

Championship. Colleagues, friends, and family all congratu-

lated the Hit Man, but when he failed to wrap his sweaty arms around his wife, Julie, she took it as a slight. But he was simply trying not to soil her new outfit.

Hart's success in the ring did not translate to a winning marriage; he and his wife were going through an extended rough patch in their relationship. Finally, on the night of Hart's championship victory over Yokozuna, Julie asked for a divorce. What should have been a joyous occasion for the Hart family turned very ugly, very quickly. "It just took the fun out of everything," says the Hit Man.

Rather than let his personal problems get in the way of his professional life, Hart sunk deeper into his work. "I had two different lives. I had the life on the road and the life at home. I was very much like Jekyll and Hyde. It never affected my performance in the ring. When things weren't going well at home, I was able to get more deeper into my matches and use that as a distraction from the things that were holding me back at home."

Unfortunately for the Hit Man, family eventually started to hold him back at work too. After brother-in-law Jim "The Anvil" Neidhart helped Owen Hart capture the prestigious *King of the Ring* crown, the two Hart outcasts placed a giant target on the back of the champ. The Hit Man wanted nothing to do with another family feud, but he sensed that Round 2 of the Bret-versus-Owen saga was unavoidable, especially with Neidhart driving the wedge between the two brothers to depths it had never reached before.

Bret and Owen ultimately agreed to square off in a Steel Cage Match at *SummerSlam*. Historically, there are a variety of reasons a rivalry escalates into a cage. In this case, it was crystal clear: The gigantic structure was to keep the warring Harts, most notably the Anvil, from interfering.

In the end, with many members of his family watching from ringside, it was Bret reaching the arena floor just moments before his brother. Upset with the result, the Anvil inexplicably attacked the British Bulldog and sister Diana from behind before going after Bret. Owen and Neidhart tossed the champion back into the cage and padlocked the door so nobody could get in. They then proceeded to decimate Bret, as a helpless Hart family gazed in horror. Brothers attempted to scale the cage, but they were knocked down each time they reached the apex. The Bulldog was finally able to get over the top and into the cage, which sent Owen and the Anvil running scared.

• • •

Brother vs. brother.

Several months into his second championship reign, the Hit Man made a random title defense against Bob Backlund on an episode of *Superstars of Wrestling*. It had been ten years since Backlund proudly wore the WWE Championship, and at age forty-four, few people actually expected him to beat the considerably younger Hart. Nonetheless, Backlund put on a stellar performance, nearly pinning the champ on several occasions before ultimately falling victim to a small package. After the match, the Hit Man extended his hand toward the normally well-mannered Backlund. Instead of shaking Hart's hand, as everybody expected, Backlund went absolutely insane. He slapped the Hit Man across the face and then locked in a painful crossface chicken wing submission hold. With a psychotic look on his face, Backlund applied more and more pressure, as officials ran to the ring to stop the carnage. Once he was pried off the champ, Backlund held his hands in front of his face and stared at them in disbelief. It was as if he was overcome by something he had no control over.

Backlund's ruthless postmatch attack led to a Submission Match for the WWE Championship at *Survivor Series*. Owen Hart was in Backlund's corner; his role was to throw in the towel at any point he believed his man couldn't continue. The British Bulldog held the same role for the champ. With Stu and Helen Hart sitting in the first row, the bell rang signifying the start of the historic first-ever Submission Match for the WWE Championship.

Toward the latter part of the contest, the Bulldog darted toward Owen, who had just interfered. Instead of running away from the charging Bulldog, Owen simply dropped to the ground as his brother-in-law went headfirst into the steel ring steps. The impact rendered the Bulldog unconscious, which meant there was nobody available to throw in the towel for Bret if needed. As the Hit Man peered over the top rope to check on the Bulldog, Backlund snuck behind the champ and cinched in the crossface chicken wing.

After several minutes seeing his brother locked in the dreaded submission hold, Owen appeared to have a change of heart. For the better part of 1994, Owen had stopped at nothing in an attempt to destroy his brother. But now that Bret was facing permanent injury, the younger Hart started to cry. "I'm sorry, Bret!" he shouted, tears rolling down his face.

Five minutes later, the Hit Man was still locked in the hold. It was becoming painfully clear that something had to be done. The match needed

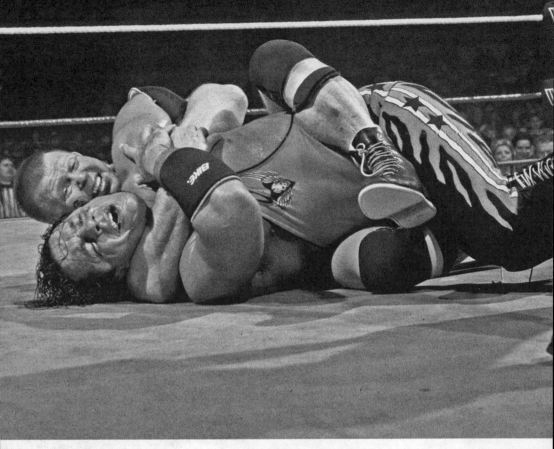

Bob Backlund vs. Bret Hart.

to be stopped. The Bulldog, however, was still out cold on the arena floor, meaning there was no way to stop the assault.

After seven minutes watching his brother writhe in pain, Owen began to plead with his parents to do something. "I didn't mean for this to happen," he wept.

Stu and Helen finally stood up and walked toward the ring. Owen handed the towel to his mother and begged for her to toss it in. Stu, realizing how important the title was to Bret, yanked the towel out of his wife's hands. For the next two minutes, the three Harts stood there helpless as Backlund applied more and more pressure to the devastating hold.

After nine minutes watching her son in the painful hold, Helen forcefully grabbed the towel back from her husband and threw it in the ring,

Bob Backlund, the new WWE champion.

signifying the end of the match, as well as Bret's eight-month WWE Championship reign.

Owen's tone immediately changed following the match. His concern turned to joy, as Backlund was presented with the WWE Championship. It was all a sham. He didn't care about his brother's well-being—only seeing his brother lose the title.

"Owen was so convincing when he was pleading with my mom to throw in the towel," remembers Bret. "And then he started jumping for joy! Fans hated it. I remember they were almost ready to pelt my parents with garbage on the way back. I think it upset my mom—she was a little caught off guard at the reaction of the fans."

16

DIESEL POWER

Bob Backlund's first WWE Championship reign will forever be remembered for its length. Unfortunately, so will his second.

A mere three days after defeating Bret Hart for the title at *Survivor Series*, Backlund lost the gold to Diesel.

Standing nearly seven feet tall and weighing over three

hundred pounds, Diesel (real name: Kevin Nash) certainly looked like a successful Superstar. Prior to his WWE debut in 1993, however, his career never really reached its full potential, largely because WCW saddled him with one horrible persona after another. He debuted as a tag team competitor named Steel. When that didn't go anywhere, they gave him silver hair and renamed him Oz (coincidentally, he was managed by Merlin the Wizard). Finally, when the Wizard and Oz failed to gain any traction, he was repackaged as mobster Vinnie Vegas. Again, the persona wasn't able to garner any positive feedback from the fans.

"When I first arrived at WCW, I was in shape and had long black hair," remembers Nash. "The first thing they did was give me a Mohawk haircut. Gee, that's brilliant—take a decent-looking guy and make him as ugly as possible right off the bat.

"There was actually a time when I was going to quit and go back to being a bouncer; I just didn't think success was going to happen. At the time, there was so much nepotism going on in WCW. Everybody had a kid that they were pushing. And if you weren't in the good ol' boys crew, you weren't going to get looked at."

Luckily, Nash stuck with it. He left WCW and signed with WWE in 1993. Shortly after inking his contract, he debuted as Shawn Michaels's bodyguard, "Big Daddy Cool" Diesel. The change of scenery was exactly what he needed. Despite spending much of his first six months in the shadow of HBK, fans could tell he would become a breakout star very shortly.

Diesel's first big break came at the 1994 *Royal Rumble*. Utilizing his size advantage, he tossed out an amazing seven Superstars, including Scott Steiner, Owen Hart, and Bob Backlund. "I remember standing there in that empty ring. There was about one minute before the next guy came in and the whole arena was chanting 'Diesel!' For the first time in my life, I thought, 'Oh my God, this is really going to happen to me.' Diesel was the s*** after that."

A few months after the *Royal Rumble*, he captured the Intercontinental Championship, defeating Razor Ramon on an episode of *Superstars*. He followed that up with a World Tag Team Championship reign, alongside HBK. Diesel's stock was rising faster than anybody had anticipated, and by year's end, he had earned a WWE Championship Match against Bob Backlund.

The match took place on November 26, 1994, at a nontelevised live event at Madison Square Garden. Those who elected to take a quick bathroom break prior to the start of the contest missed witnessing history. After a kick to the midsection and a Jackknife powerbomb, Diesel covered Backlund for the win. In all, the match lasted eight seconds.

"The feeling of being announced as WWE Champion for the first time is unexplainable. I was the champion of the federation I used to watch on television. I was a huge Hogan fan, and now I had the same title as Hulk. To me, it was a moment in my career like no other. And the fact that it was in the Garden made it even more special for me."

Diesel's in-ring celebration was one of pure jubilation. After barely breaking a sweat, he held the title high, much to the delight of the thousands in attendance at MSG. Once he got home, however, Diesel was only concerned about satisfying one person. "I think everybody at one time or another has put the title on nude. And I guarantee every winner has walked up to their wife and said, 'Honey, you're getting a night with the champ.' Maybe I'm the only one."

At the time of Diesel's win over Backlund, he was only sixteen months into his fulltime wrestling career. Despite being with WCW for three years, his lack of success meant he was only needed to compete about thirty-five times a year. So much of the early portion of his WWE Championship reign was on-the-job training. Luckily for him, he had a stellar supporting cast around him. On a nightly basis, he was climbing into the ring with Shawn Michaels, Razor Ramon, or Undertaker. It was nearly impossible for him to have a bad match against such great competition.

In his first major title defense, Diesel battled former WWE Champion Bret Hart at the 1995 *Royal Rumble*. Both Superstars were extremely popular at the time and had a great deal of respect for each other. Too bad the rest of the roster didn't share that same respect: On three separate occasions, the match was forced to stop after outside interference from other Superstars, including HBK, Owen Hart, and Jeff Jarrett. The third stoppage of action proved to be the last. Unable to control the mayhem any longer, the referee ordered the match to end, with Diesel retaining the title.

In retrospect, the contest did little to earn much historical meaning. But history was eventually made later that same night when Shawn Michaels became the first Superstar to go wire-to-wire to win the *Royal*

Rumble. The victory earned him a spot in his first *WrestleMania* main event against former friend and WWE Champion Diesel.

"We worked so much together prior to *WrestleMania,* but never really against each other," says Diesel. "Then we were in Europe and we had a couple matches before coming home toward *'Mania.* We were just missing a little something in those matches. Then we worked together in Berlin. It was about thirty minutes and it was *dead-on.* Shawn had great matches with Scott [Hall] and all the other guys, but this was our first great match."

According to Diesel, they were unable to re-create the same magic when they battled at *WrestleMania XI.* Nonetheless, Big Daddy Cool was able to defeat Michaels with a Jackknife powerbomb.

Following *WrestleMania,* Diesel steamrolled over HBK's other former bodyguard, Sid, in a Lumberjack Match at *In Your House 2,* and he picked up a decisive victory over King Mabel at *SummerSlam.* At the time, *SummerSlam* was one of WWE's "big five" Pay-Per-Views (*Royal Rumble, WrestleMania, King of the Ring,* and *Survivor Series* were the others), which meant a big payday for the champ. "I bought a 1993 Bronco with my *SummerSlam* check. And I still have that same Bronco—I was never able to drive an exotic because of my size."

By late 1995, Diesel had earned the distinction of being the longest-running WWE Champion since Hulk Hogan's second reign, which started in April 1989. Unfortunately for "Big Daddy Cool," however, his epic title reign would never see the new year. On November 19, 1995, just one week shy of his one-year anniversary of becoming WWE Champion, Diesel lost the gold to Bret Hart in a No Disqualification Match at *Survivor Series.* The lax rules made for a brutal battle, one that present-day fans might call a Hardcore Match. It was this unique atmosphere that helped make the contest so memorable, even years later.

HART: I always thought it was Kevin Nash's greatest match. He told me that it was the best one he ever had. It was a really good ending. It was before the hardcore endings you see today. It really did catch everybody by surprise. And before that, nobody expected me to go crashing through a table. I can honestly say that table didn't have

Bret Hart and Diesel get hardcore.

any give. When I go back and watch it, as soon as I went through the
table, you can see the whole crowd rise up at the railing. They knew
that something monumental had just happened.

If you were a fan of Kevin Nash or Bret Hart, the match lived
up to all expectations. It was a closely fought dogfight that made you
respect both of us at the end.

DIESEL: To this day, it's one of my three favorite matches I've ever had. I never had a bad one with Bret. A lot of people might not remember, but the chair shot I gave Bret on the floor was probably the first effective one that WWE had seen in sixteen months. So when I reared back that chair and whacked him, the fans didn't know how to react.

All these years later, I find it funny that people say they never had a good relationship with Bret. I think they just misunderstood him. He was very much a lone wolf, but he had a great sense of humor, very dry and sarcastic. We always had great respect for each other. And he was a pro. There was never a time when he didn't lace 'em up. You knew if you were in there with Bret, you were going to have a great match.

Six months after losing the title to Bret Hart, Diesel made the difficult choice to leave WWE for WCW. With his wife eight months pregnant, and him always being on the road with WWE, he eventually chose WCW's lighter workload. "Plus, the Turner organization threw a ton of money at me and Scott [Hall]."

17

BOYHOOD NIGHTMARE?

As WWE charged toward *WrestleMania XII*, it started to become clear that Shawn Michaels could no longer be denied
his spot at the top of the roster. After more than a decade
of tag team success, Intercontinental Championship reigns,
and amazing innovations such as the Ladder Match, the

general feeling was that the Heartbreak Kid would soon become WWE Champion.

Michaels's big opportunity finally came when he eliminated Diesel to win the 1996 *Royal Rumble*. The victory marked HBK's second straight Rumble triumph and effectively solidified a spot at *WrestleMania*, where he would challenge Bret Hart.

Recognizing the white-hot popularity of Michaels at the time, WWE's marketing machine began a highly publicized campaign promoting HBK's boyhood dream of one day capturing the WWE title. They told the story of a twelve-year-old Shawn who wanted nothing more than to be like the godly champions he saw each week on television. His original trainer, Jose Lothario, was even brought in to help him prepare. Vignettes of the two training in dingy San Antonio locales were shot, and while many insiders scoffed at the idea of having somebody in his sixties training a young man in peak physical condition, HBK wanted it no other way. Lothario played a major role in the early successes of Michaels, and he wanted to repay him by making him a part of the biggest show of the year, *WrestleMania*.

Prior to *WrestleMania XII,* no *WrestleMania* main event had ever reached the twenty-five-minute mark. So when longtime WWE employee Pat Patterson came up with the idea of a sixty-minute Iron Man Match, many were naturally skeptical. But WWE eventually saw it as an opportunity to showcase a revolutionary new match on their grandest stage.

As a result of the decision to hold an Iron Man Match, Shawn Michaels and Bret Hart were forced to spend the next several weeks preparing their bodies for the hell they were about to endure. At the time, Michaels's schedule allowed for slightly more time off than his opponent, which meant more time to increase his cardio workouts. Hart, however, was forced to prepare for *WrestleMania* while simultaneously fulfilling his endless commitments as WWE Champion. In addition to making public appearances, the Hit Man was on the road every night. His competition at the time was usually Diesel, Undertaker, or Yokozuna—three men who weren't necessarily ideal opponents for somebody looking to increase his endurance.

"So I started doing a really strong cardio program early in the day," said Hart. "I would exhaust myself, then go back to my room and lie down, and then I would go to the arena and wrestle. It was like having two-a-days in football. I was mostly riding the stationary bike for an hour at full blast every single day. Then I would go full blast in my matches. This was on top of my normal workout. I never trained harder for anything."

By the time of *WrestleMania*, both Superstars were in the best shape of their lives. Moments before the match, Shawn Michaels theatrically descended from the Arrowhead Pond ceiling via zipline, while Bret Hart placed his signature sunglasses on the head of his six-year-old son, Blade. Before the opening bell even rang, both men had already given the fans *WrestleMania* moments that would live forever. The match itself didn't disappoint, either. Amazingly, after sixty minutes of nonstop action, neither man had been able to win a fall. This resulted in WWE President Gorilla Monsoon ordering the match to continue under sudden-death rules.

Despite Hart controlling the majority of sudden-death, HBK somehow mustered up enough energy to land Sweet Chin Music. The Hit Man crashed to the mat, as an exhausted Michaels fell on top of his opponent. Three seconds later, Shawn Michaels was WWE Champion.

As an emotional Michaels dropped to his knees hugging his newly won WWE Championship, Vince McMahon jubilantly announced to a worldwide audience watching on Pay-Per-View that the boyhood dream had come true. Little did anybody know, though, that while it appeared that Michaels was celebrating in the ring, his inner thoughts were far from festive.

"I felt all by myself," he says, more than thirteen years after the match. "I felt this way many times, but especially on this night. I was in front of 20,000 people and I don't know how many more watching on Pay-Per-View, but I felt all alone. I suppose in some respect, it's kind of sad. I felt a little vindicated and proud of what I had done, but at the same time, all the pressure in the world was on me. It was a bittersweet situation."

Unlike the Superstar fans see today, the 1996 version of Shawn Michaels was a self-admitted irrational conspiracy theorist, who never believed the company was truly behind him. Instead, he assumed his title reign was nothing but a test to see if he had what it took. And his flammable attitude at the time didn't make things any easier. Outside of a select few, there weren't many who cared for HBK.

"Being the heat-seeker that I was, I knew there were a number of people hoping for me to fail," says Michaels of his reign. "On top of that, I had the pressure to draw money and ratings. It's a pretty unwinnable situation because the credit gets spread around the company when something good happens, but when things aren't going right, the blame is always on the guy wearing the title. As the champ, everybody was looking to me to draw money for their families, while at the same time hoping I would stumble and fall. It was a tough spot to be in."

Despite the feelings of emptiness and the pressures of being WWE Champion, Michaels continued to wow audiences with his in-ring ability. In April, he defeated Diesel in a match that quickly turned ugly. At one point, Big Daddy Cool powerbombed HBK directly through the ringside announcers' table. The devastation of the move left the audience in awe, but it was what happened moments later that proved most memorable. While sitting ringside for the event, legendary AWA wrestler "Mad Dog" Vachon had his prosthetic leg ripped from his body by Diesel. The challenger tried to use it as a weapon, but Michaels was able to gather the artificial limb and use it first, which was followed by Sweet Chin Music for the win.

According to Diesel, it was Pat Patterson who reminded him prior to the match that Vachon was walking on a possible weapon and that he would be sitting ringside. By night's end, the sight of Michaels using Vachon's prosthetic leg, coupled with his ability to rebound from such a brutal beating, provided one of the first truly memorable moments of HBK's reign.

Over the next several months, Michaels recorded victories over much larger competition, including the British Bulldog and Vader. But despite the wins in the ring, the stress was continuing to mount. WCW's *Monday Nitro* had begun its eighty-four-week reign atop the Monday night TV ratings war, which caused some to question HBK's ability to bring WWE back to the top. This just further infuriated an already combustible Michaels, who responded by verbally attacking anybody in the locker room on a regular basis. In his mind, there was no way he was the problem for WWE's perceived inadequacies; he was putting on some of the best matches of all time. So everybody else felt his wrath.

Part of WWE's problem at the time, according to Michaels, was that they were not cutting edge enough. WCW had the New World Order. They had Kevin Nash and Scott Hall, as well as the newly dubbed "Hollywood" Hogan, who had just turned his back on the fans. They were doing the unthinkable, while Michaels was traveling the country with his elderly trainer, smiling ear to ear for his Kliq.

In September 1996, Michaels had the opportunity to briefly scratch his itch to be edgy when he faced the deranged Mankind (Mick Foley) at *In Your House: Mind Games*. Mankind's maniacal fighting style gave HBK the excuse he needed to turn up the volume and do some brawling, as opposed to pure wrestling. In the end, it was Michaels winning via disqualification after Vader ran in and attacked the champ. Despite the loss, Foley later praised HBK in his book *Have a Nice Day*, for carrying him to such a great match.

"I too have always been proud of that match," claims Michaels. "And I have to give a ton of the credit to Mick because at that time, I was so Goody Two-shoes. But his character brought some really different perspectives to the match, which made HBK more aggressive. I was doing things that I wouldn't have ordinarily done. There was a more rugged aspect to the match. That's always been one of my personal favorites because it wasn't a rank-and-file Shawn Michaels performance."

Surprisingly, a Pay-Per-View rematch was never announced, despite this being relatively common practice following a disqualification in a match of such magnitude. Instead, Shawn Michaels entered into a rivalry with Sycho Sid, who beat Vader at *In Your House: Buried Alive* to become the number-one contender for HBK's title.

Sid was a mountain of a man, who some say never really reached his full potential during his first run with WWE in the early 1990s. But since returning in 1995, his fortunes began to change. It wasn't uncommon to see Sid in main events opposite the likes of Diesel or Vader. And on November 16, 1996, he found himself in yet another main event. This time he was challenging HBK for the WWE Championship at *Survivor Series* at Madison Square Garden.

The match will forever be remembered for the reaction Shawn Michaels received from the fans. For years, the MSG crowd had been ahead of the curve. If they didn't like somebody, they let it be known, regardless of whether every other arena in the world cheered that person.

On this night, they didn't like Shawn Michaels.

His smiling good-guy routine had grown old with them, and for the first time in years he was showered with boos. The crowd response resulted in a negative reaction from HBK, who began to antagonize the audience even more. At one point, he even sarcastically signaled for more boos. For fans of Michaels, the sight of him playing the bad guy certainly was surreal.

"I know people thought I lost my cool that night," explains HBK. "But the truth is, I responded naturally to how they responded to me. The emotional part of the business has always been very real. Some people thought I shouldn't have let it get to me, but that's just silly. That's like having somebody slap you in the face and you turn around and walk away. That's not something I do.

"The business was changing then anyway. I knew that the guy they liked was a lot more rugged than they were allowing me to be. On that particular night, in front of that crowd, they felt the good guy was a dweeb and that Sid was cool. I felt that I should respond accordingly. I suppose some people would disagree . . . but at that time, I was emotional and reactionary. I always did what I thought was natural. Anything else is less real, and when it's less real, people know."

With the raucous crowd backing the challenger, Sid assaulted Jose Lothario with a television camera. A distraught Shawn Michaels quickly ran to his mentor's aide, but while tending to Lothario, he too was hit by a camera-wielding Sid. Moments later, Sid delivered a bone-shattering

powerbomb and covered Michaels for the win. Eight months after Michaels had achieved his boyhood dream, his world was crumbling around him. Not only did he lose the WWE Championship, but he also lost the most influential crowd in the world—the one at Madison Square Garden.

Sid, despite the victory, wasn't in a much better place mentally. Unlike the select few before him who were lucky enough to proudly call themselves WWE Champions, Sid actually saw it as a burden.

"I didn't want the extra weight of the title to carry around," admits Sid nearly a decade and a half later. "I actually tried to keep it with the ring crew because I didn't want it in my bag. I never went home and showed it off and I never took pictures with it. Plus, being champion really just increased my workload. That's all.

"I look at the business differently than a lot of other people. I don't look at wins and losses and title reigns. If you won the title fourteen times, you lost it fifteen times. I was brought up in smaller territories where you weren't going to see the title because it was always on Jerry Lawler or Robert Fuller. So we didn't *expect* titles."

Luckily for Sid, he wasn't tasked with lugging the gold around for very long. Just two months into his reign, he lost the title to HBK at the *Royal Rumble* in a match that took place in Michaels's hometown of San Antonio, Texas.

"I had a lot of friends from high school there that night," says Michaels. "It was important to me because it was the first real dome show that we had done in a long time, and it was important to me to have the place full. I was really enamored by performing in front of my friends in a 60,000-seat dome."

To help fill the monstrous venue, WWE launched a massive Texas-based marketing campaign, urging fans to come out and support their home-state hero. It was one of the rare times in history that the challenger was used as the main marketing tool over the champion.

Sid shrugged it off. "If they thought Shawn was more marketable than me, that's fine," he says. "They know the business part of the business better than I do. You can't be offended by that. I'm a different person than most of the other guys. I never looked at a wrestling magazine, never read a dirt sheet. If you're looking for accolades there, then you're in the wrong business. I learned that in my first year when I was Lord Humongous. Some

Shawn Michaels vs. Sid.

dirt sheet said, 'Who is that doing the Lord Humongous gimmick? He's the worst Lord Humongous of all time.' Robert Fuller was the booker and a good friend of mine, and he told me not to look at those things again. And ever since then, I haven't."

With the title back in his possession, HBK appeared poised for another lengthy WWE Championship run. But shortly after regaining the gold, a casual trip home turned fateful and eventually altered the course of Shawn Michaels's career.

"I went to see my mom," recalls HBK. "At the time, a lot of people didn't like me. I was tired and run-down. She finally turned to me and said, 'You don't smile anymore. You've lost your smile.'"

Three weeks later, Michaels would use those same words in what would turn out to be one of WWE's most historic interviews. But first, he had to get his injured knee examined.

"I had gone to just a general orthopedic in San Antonio. This was before we had Dr. James Andrews. The guy in San Antonio didn't know anything about our line of work. He looked at me and said, 'With a knee like that, you're done. You'll never wrestle again.' I thought, 'I'm only thirty-two years old and it's all over.'"

On February 13, 1997, a somber Michaels broke the bad news to the public in an interview with Vince McMahon on *Raw*: "Over the past couple of months, there's been a lot of talk of people having bad attitudes and a lot revolving around this belt," said HBK as he looked down at the WWE Championship. "All I know today is that one thing that is not going to revolve around this belt for a long time is going to be Shawn Michaels. I don't know where I'm at right now. I have to have everything checked. I may be beyond reconstructive knee surgery. I may or may not be able to fix it, but if I can't come back and perform at the level I performed at before, I can't perform. I can't come out here and just go half-assed. I have to come out here and I have to romp and stomp and I have to get tossed around. I have to toss people around and I have to have fun.

"The schedule over the past year I took on because I didn't feel like I could say no. I wanted to do everything. I wanted to enjoy my life as the champion. I wanted to ride in Learjets and I wanted to ride in limousines. I wanted to be on TV shows and I wanted to do autograph sessions.

And I got to do every bit of that. If nothing else, I have all of that to take with me.

"I know right now we are in the middle of a time where toughness is real big here in WWE. And unfortunately, all I've got for you right now is a lot of sorrow, a lot of tears, and a lot of emotion. I don't have any toughness for anybody. So I guess, here you go. Here's your belt," said HBK, handing over the WWE Championship.

"What I'm going to do is go back home and see what's left for me, whether it be in this ring, whether it be out of this ring," continued Michaels, thinking back to the words his mother told him three weeks earlier. "I know that over the last several months, I've lost a lot of things, and one of them has been my smile. And I know it doesn't mean a whole lot to everybody else, but it means a lot to me. So I have to go back and fix myself, and take care of myself, and I have to go back and I have to find my smile, because somewhere along the line I lost it. I don't care if it's unpopular. I don't care if people want to make fun of me because I'm an emotional guy. But this is all I ever wanted to do, and over the last year, I got to do it."

Tears began to fall down Michaels's face as he struggled to continue.

"Whether you like me or not, I just want to tell you that last year was the most wonderful year of my life, and if I never get to do it again, it'll be okay because I got to live one full year as being the number-one guy in this business. It was the single most greatest year of my life. And I have you to thank, and I have everybody here to thank. And it means a lot to me. I'm going to go home now."

An emotional Shawn Michaels rode off into the sunset, not knowing if he would ever lace up a pair of boots again. To this day, many of his macho peers still poke fun at him for being so emotional during the "lost smile" interview.

"It was something my mom said and something I knew was true," recalls Michaels. "I was miserable, so I said it. People bring that line up to me and it's supposed to bother me, but it doesn't. I was a miserable son of a bitch . . . life was horrible. Everything isn't about wrestling. It took me twenty years to figure that out. That's sad. Anybody who thinks like that is silly. I'd rather be real than convince some jackoff in a gym that I'm a bad S.O.B."

But was HBK really being real? Longtime rival Bret Hart thought Michaels was faking to avoid having to defend the title against him. Hart recalls the moment in his 2007 autobiography, *Hitman*: "He walked out without so much as a limp and with the heartbreaking trickle of the occasional tear, he talked of having lived his dream. Fans jeered him, so the cameras cut to close-ups of girls crying. He said he simply had to listen to his doctors. He'd not only hurt his knee, he had 'lost his smile' over the last few months and was going home to find it. Every wrestler standing with me rolled his eyes as Shawn forfeited the title, handing the belt to Vince, who was caked in makeup and looked peculiarly Dracula-like as he too appeared to be fighting back tears. I'd worked a Tag Team Match with Shawn at the Meadowlands only three days before, and there was nothing wrong with his knee."

The day after HBK surrendered the WWE Championship, McMahon called him and urged him to see noted orthopedic surgeon Dr. James Andrews in Alabama. After examining the leg, Dr. Andrews agreed that it was in bad shape, but he told Michaels he could still perform if he could withstand the pain, wear a brace, and go through an extensive rehab process. The sudden change in diagnosis did little to help convince the naysayers that the injury was legitimate.

"I know people thought at the time I was trying to be disingenuous and swerve people. But I've never really had a lot of foresight into anything I do. Most of the stuff I've done in my career has been on emotion and reaction. I don't put a whole lot of contemplated forethought into anything. I don't really have that ability. I don't like to overthink anything. I think life is pretty simple and I think our business is pretty simple. I tend to think if you overthink any of it, you just complicate it. I've managed to create a successful career on emotion and reaction, so I figured I would just go with that as opposed to something else."

Legitimate or not, Michaels's title reign was over, and WWE was left scrambling for a new champion.

18

DARK DAZE

On the morning of February 13, 1997, members of the WWE front office woke up satisfied with the thought of Shawn Michaels being their top Superstar. At the time, HBK was only one month into his reign, but it was imagined that he would bring some much needed stability back to the title—

something rival WCW was very much experiencing at the time with Hollywood Hogan, who was in the middle of a one-year reign. But when they walked into the arena later that day, those once-pleased officials were blindsided with terrible news: HBK would never wrestle again, according to doctors in San Antonio. Believing they were left with no other choice, WWE and Shawn Michaels agreed that it would be best if he surrendered the title.

The move left WWE, three days away from a Pay-Per-View, scrambling for a solution to fill the sudden vacancy. They ultimately decided to award the title to the winner of a Four Corners Elimination Match at *In Your House: Final Four.* By night's end, Bret Hart had outlasted Stone Cold Steve Austin, Vader, and Undertaker to claim his fourth WWE Championship. But the victory did little to restore stability to the title; just one night later, Sycho Sid capitalized on some outside interference from Steve Austin to dethrone the Hit Man.

With the loss, Hart became the owner of one of the shortest reigns in WWE Championship history. At the time, only Andre the Giant and Yokozuna claimed less lengthy reigns.

"I almost don't even count it," says Hart, looking back. "It was my fourth reign. That's all it was—just a number."

While the reign itself certainly failed to live up to his lofty standards, the Hit Man can look back and appreciate how the loss helped refresh his character. In the weeks following the defeat, Hart began to complain about being cheated out of the WWE Championship. For years, he had carried himself as the proud competitor, win or lose. But since the loss to Sycho Sid, his objections had become mildly annoying. Fans slowly began to turn on him. He wasn't quite an official villain yet, but he was clearly moving in that direction.

"For me to lose the title the way that I did was really powerful," claims Hart. "There was a lot of drama in that match against Sid. When they screwed me out of the title that night, it did a lot for me. I realized then that I didn't need the title. It was just what I needed to rejuvenate my character at the time."

Over the next several weeks, a revitalized Bret Hart blurred the lines between villain and hero. His rival Stone Cold Steve Austin did the same. They eventually squared off at *WrestleMania 13,* where their roles were officially clarified. Longtime fan favorite Hart completely lost the support of his followers when he brutally bloodied Austin to the point of unconsciousness, then attacked him even more after the match. Stone Cold won over his former detractors when he refused to quit, despite the great loss of blood. The match marked one of the rare moments where the fans switched their allegiances over the course of the contest for not just one but both Superstars.

Sycho Sid was inked to defend his newly won WWE Championship against Undertaker in a No Disqualification Match at *WrestleMania 13*. Before this could happen, though, both Shawn Michaels and Bret Hart did all they could to redirect the focus on themselves.

Six days prior to *WrestleMania*, HBK returned from his controversial injury to announce he had found his smile. "And you'll never guess where it was," he joked. "It was back in San Antonio, Texas, where I left it. But now I decided to bring it with me wherever I go." He then went on to proclaim how miffed he was that he wasn't invited to *WrestleMania* . . . so he invited himself to be part of the commentating team for the WWE Championship Match.

Bret Hart, WWE's newest villain, also tried his hand at stealing the spotlight. Just moments before the start of the main event, the Hit Man purposefully walked to the ring and grabbed a microphone.

"First of all, you phony little faker," he said, staring at HBK. "Why don't you take your little pussyfoot injury and go back and find your smile. But whatever you do, stay out of this match." He then complained about being screwed out of his championship before calling Sid a fraud.

The WWE Champion had heard enough. He powerbombed Bret Hart and sent him back to the locker room. But that was not the last anybody would see of the Hit Man. Twenty minutes later, Hart ran to the ring yet again in an attempt to spoil a physical classic between two of WWE's best big men. His attendance at ringside distracted Sid long enough for Undertaker to scoop the champ up and drop him on his head via the Tombstone Piledriver. The impact of the move gave the Deadman more than enough time to dramatically cross Sid's arms across his chest and cover him for the win. For the first time since briefly holding the title in 1991, the Phenom was back on top as WWE Champion. At the time, the five-plus years in

Sid vs. Undertaker,
WrestleMania 13

between his reigns marked the second longest stretch a champion had to wait before regaining the title.

Unlike Undertaker's first WWE title victory over Hulk Hogan in 1991, Paul Bearer was not in the Deadman's corner at *WrestleMania 13* when he toppled Sid. Several months earlier, Bearer shocked the wrestling world when he turned on Undertaker in favor of aligning with the deranged Mankind. And now that the Phenom was occupying WWE's top spot, Bearer became obsessed with doing all he could to ruin the life of his former protégé, including revealing an unthinkable secret.

PAUL BEARER TELLS HIS SECRET IN AN INTERVIEW WITH VINCE McMAHON: We're going to have to go back a few years, Mr. McMahon. About twenty years to be exact. We're talking about a little funeral home, sitting up on a hill, beautiful oak trees all around, and a wonderful, wonderful family-owned funeral home. The family lived upstairs. The father was a mortician, who ran the funeral home. The mother was a secretary, the receptionist. But there were two little kids there. One kid was a little redheaded punk. And then there was a second kid, a sweet little kid named Kane.

I was the apprentice at the funeral home. I worked under the redheaded punk's father, who by now you probably know is Undertaker. Undertaker's father was a mortician of excellence. He taught me everything I know. He taught me the correct way to prepare a body for burial, how to do the makeup, how to deal with the families. He taught me from A to Z. But while I was working at that funeral home, I saw a lot of things going on that shouldn't have been happening. This little redheaded punk, there was something funny about him. He had a look in his eyes. The look of the devil! He was the devil's seed, if you know what I mean.

What was so sad about the whole situation is that poor little Kane, the little brother, followed Undertaker around everywhere he went. Undertaker was little Kane's hero. Anything Undertaker did was fine. Well, it went on for about two years, my apprenticeship. I was

going to college at night, taking courses in mortuary science at the same time.

Undertaker and Kane would run around the funeral home like wild men. They had free rein of the property. They'd sneak out behind the garage. I saw what they were doing. Their momma and daddy didn't see what they were doing, but I saw what they were doing. I saw them taking chemicals out of the embalming room of the funeral home. I saw them sneaking behind the garage, smoking cigarettes when they were little kids.

But you know, one particular afternoon, I was leaving to go to school. As I backed my car out of the funeral home, I looked behind, and who do I see? That redheaded devil seed Undertaker with his little brother. Something was funny, something didn't seem right. But I went ahead and backed out of the driveway and went to school. I came back from school about ten o'clock that night, and what do I see? I see fire trucks. I see ambulances. I see steam and smoke. And I see the funeral home in ashes. Someone burned down the funeral home. Inside the funeral home was this lovely family that took care of me. I looked over to the bushes. Who did I see in the bushes? Undertaker! Undertaker, you burnt the funeral home to the ground. And along with the funeral home, you killed your parents. You killed your family, Undertaker! I know it. I've had this secret on my inside all my life. Twenty years. You killed them. Undertaker, you are a murderer! You are a murderer, Undertaker!

WWE fans refused to give any credence to Bearer's chilling story. But then Undertaker awed the wrestling world when he revealed that the life-altering event did, in fact, happen. But Bearer's version, according to the Phenom, was filled with only half-truths.

UNDERTAKER'S VERSION OF THE STORY: It's true. Yes, it is true. My mother, my father, and my little brother burned to death in the family funeral home. But I think it's important that we have all the facts straight. Yes, Kane and I were playing with matches that day. And we were punished when my father found us. Me more so than

Kane: I was the oldest, I should've known better. My father explained to us what we were doing and how those liquids were flammable.

After he punished me, he sent me on my way to do my daily chores. And as I was leaving the funeral home, I looked back and I saw Kane leaving out of one of the rear doors of the embalming room. And I saw that he had those liquids in his hand. It never occurred to me what he was going to do. I thought nothing of it. And I live with that fact every day of my life.

Kane was my responsibility. He was my little brother. As I returned to the funeral home from doing my chores, I could hear the sirens. I could see the smoke filling the sky. Without knowing, I knew. I knew what had happened. And I ran, and I ran as fast as I could. When I got to the funeral home, it was engulfed in flames. I never slowed down for one second. I ran right for the front door. That's when they grabbed me. They wouldn't let me go in. The firefighters, they held me back. And as I stood there restrained, I watched the funeral home. And inside that funeral home was my mother, my father, and little Kane.

I watched that funeral home burn down to the ground. And yes, Paul, it's true: I wasn't at the funeral. But you didn't care to explain to the people why that was . . . That two nights before, during the middle of the night, you dragged me to the neighboring funeral home so that I could see my family. Until this very day, the image of my mother lying on that table . . . As you pulled that sheet back, and I looked at the burnt and charred body of the most wonderful woman that had ever walked on this earth lying there, the air escaped from my lungs. I couldn't breathe. I thought I was going to be sick. But you insisted, you insisted that this small boy in the middle of the night go and look at the charred remains of what two days earlier was his family. It was a day that changed me forever.

For me to be able to deal with the death of my family, I had to look at death. I had to understand that without death, there cannot be life. So I had taken it upon myself to walk a path where no one else chooses to. I draw strength from the spirit of the dead, and the spirit of my mother, of my father, and of my little brother will strike you down, Paul Bearer. Will strike you down!

Both versions of the story were filled with gruesome depictions of death. However, while Undertaker's fatalities totaled three, Bearer's only reached two—the mother and father. According to Bearer, Undertaker's brother was still alive. He was charred and scarred, but still very much breathing.

Despite being armed with the astonishing news that his little brother may, in fact, be alive after so many years, Undertaker somehow shelved his emotions and entered into battle with Hart at *SummerSlam*. After spending the past several months fending off such physical behemoths as Sid, Vader, and Mankind, the Deadman knew this match would be much different.

"I think in a lot of ways, Undertaker wanted to work with somebody like me," reflects Bret Hart. "He was always working with Giant Gonzales and those types of guys at the time. By working with me he was able to show everybody that he could actually wrestle. Throughout the 1990s, Undertaker and myself were the two biggest stars in the company, and to finally see us wrestle at *SummerSlam* was a dream match for a lot of fans."

Following an errant chair shot by guest referee Shawn Michaels, Hart dropped on top of Undertaker for the pin. HBK looked on in disbelief for a brief moment before finally realizing he had to do the right thing and count the Phenom's shoulders to the mat, otherwise he would no longer be allowed to wrestle in the United States, as per the prematch stipulations. In the end, Michaels did do the right thing, and as a result, Undertaker's nearly five-month reign came to an end.

"We left it all out on the field that night. After the match, I went back to the dressing room and my son Blade was helping me take my gear off. I was so sore and so beaten that I could barely undo the laces of my boots. I felt like I was run over by a train. You know when you gave everything you had in a match—that was one of those times."

After *SummerSlam*, Undertaker sought retribution against Shawn Michaels in the first-ever Hell in a Cell Match at *Badd Blood*. During the contest, Paul Bearer's mind games finally came to a head when a disfigured monster emerged from the locker room.

It was Kane.

A shocked Undertaker peered into the face of his little brother. Before the Phenom could fully grasp the enormity of what was happening, Kane unleashed twenty years of pent-up rage and frustration on his big brother, even hitting him with his own signature Tombstone Piledriver.

Over the next thirteen years, the brothers went on to experience one of history's rockiest relationships, complete with fiery rivalries and unlikely unions, resulting in WWE and WCW Tag Team Championship reigns.

Meanwhile, Hart was reveling in his latest WWE Championship victory.

"I remember thinking then, and I still do today, that the last title win against Undertaker was as good as it ever got with me. Of course, you can never top the first one. Winning the title the first time gave me permission to say 'I am the best there is, the best there was, the best there ever will be.' But the fifth win was such a better match, the great one I always wanted to have. It's one of my favorite matches of all time."

19

MONTREAL SCREWJOB

Bret Hart was on top of the world following his *SummerSlam* victory over Undertaker in August 1997. Not only did he finally have the quality title match he desired for so long, but he also tied Hulk Hogan's then-record of five WWE Championship reigns. Coupled with the security of a newly signed twenty-year WWE contract, things couldn't have been going any better for the Hit Man. Or so he thought.

About six weeks after *SummerSlam*, Hart was ordered to Vince McMahon's office for a meeting. According to Hart, McMahon claimed that WCW's dominance over WWE was sending his company into financial peril. As a result, he intended on breaching Hart's contract ($10.5 million over twenty years). Instead of paying him his full salary, McMahon informed his champion he would receive his money at the back end of his lengthy deal. The meeting ended with McMahon urging Hart to see if he could get WCW to offer him the same deal they offered him the year before when he was a free agent: $9 million over three years. If Hart could successfully ink a deal with WCW, WWE would no longer be responsible for the $10.5 million owed to the Hit Man. McMahon gave Hart until November 1 to negotiate a contract with WCW.

Heeding his boss's advice, Hart reached out to WCW to see if the same deal was on the table. They came back with $7.5 million over three years—almost as much as McMahon was giving him over twenty years. Despite the large amount of money, though, Hart's home was in the WWE ring. "I never had any intention of leaving," says Hart. "Naively enough, I thought whatever was happening with me and Vince would get sorted out."

Hart claims to have called McMahon on October 31, to discuss his WWE future and ultimately inform him that he would not be taking WCW's deal. They spoke only briefly before McMahon told the Hit Man he would call him back later with a detailed outline of his future. According to Hart, the call didn't come until minutes before the midnight deadline, and to make matters worse, the conversation turned somewhat sour when McMahon's outline was not to Hart's liking. Before hanging up, McMahon told his champion to think with his head and take the security of the WCW deal.

Moments later, Hart signed his WCW contract and faxed it back to Eric Bischoff. Just like that, his fourteen-year WWE career was over.

With his champion's signature on the rival's contract, Vince McMahon had to do everything in his power to ensure another Alundra Blayze incident wasn't on the horizon. In December 1995, WWE Women's Champion Blayze

Jim Neidhart and Owen Hart console Bret Hart.

abruptly left to sign with WCW. In her initial appearance on *Monday Nitro,* the buxom blonde held up the WWE Women's title she once proudly carried and proceeded to throw it into a garbage can. The sight of a WWE titlist disrespecting WWE on WCW television remains one of the most infamous moments in sports-entertainment history. In an attempt to avoid another embarrassing situation, McMahon wanted Hart to lose the WWE Championship to Shawn Michaels at *Survivor Series* in Montreal, Canada. This would eliminate any chances of the Hit Man showing up on *Nitro* with the WWE title. The last thing Hart wanted to do, however, was lose the gold in his home country.

Considering McMahon's powerful position, a fan could assume Vince would simply demand that Hart surrender the gold to Michaels at *Survivor Series.* This was not the case, though. Hart's contract stated that he had full creative control over the final thirty days of his term. And as luck would have it, the Hit Man had no plans of walking out of Canada without his WWE Championship.

During this time period, McMahon held weekly conference calls with Triple H and Shawn Michaels. On the Wednesday before *Survivor Series*, he alerted both Superstars to Hart's unwillingness to surrender the gold. Being the true historians of the game that they were, both Triple H and HBK grew irate over the news. To them, doing what was asked of you on your way out the door of a promotion has always been a time-honored tradition. Every competitor who has ever laced a pair of boots lived by this rule. To hear that Hart was refusing to honor McMahon's wishes offended Triple H and HBK.

In his 2005 autobiography, *Heartbreak and Triumph*, Michaels recalls his exchange with McMahon during the conference call: "I'll do whatever you want. We'll just take it off him. I'll just swerve him or whatever I have to. You tell me what needs to get done. You and this company have put up with so much from me. My loyalty is here with you. I'll do whatever you want."

"What are you talking about, Shawn?"

"Whatever it takes. If we have to do a fast count or get him in a hold and tell someone to ring the bell, I'll do whatever you want me to do."

"That's pretty serious. That has to be a last resort. I still have until Saturday to talk to Bret. That may have to be a real option. This cannot be discussed with anyone. Pat [Patterson] can't know—nobody can know about this but the three of us right now."

Saturday came and Hart still refused to give in to the demands. As a result, Vince McMahon and Shawn Michaels felt they had very little choice.

Early on Sunday, the day of *Survivor Series*, HBK came up with the plan to get Hart in a Sharpshooter. Once it was locked in, referee Earl Hebner, who would be tipped off prior to the start of the match, would immediately call for the bell. And just like that, the unsuspecting Bret Hart would see his fifth title reign, as well as his WWE career, come to an embarrassing end.

Michaels and Hart shared a private moment together prior to the start of the Pay-Per-View. This was wildly uncharacteristic, considering the ill feelings both men developed for each other over the years. Perhaps Hart, realizing the end was near, was trying to extend an olive branch before departing for WCW. Either way, their exchange did not resonate well with

HBK, who was forced to feign compassion, knowing that he was about to screw Hart out of his most prized possession.

"It was the most uncomfortable talk ever," remembers Michaels. "He and I had a lot of conversations over the years . . . mending and breaking down, mending and breaking down. And on this day, we had another one. I never felt lower. We shook hands and I knew full well what was going on. I look back at it now and I feel like a scumbag."

But there was no turning back for Shawn Michaels. He had a job to do: take the WWE Championship from Bret Hart. Everything went according to HBK's plan during the bout. Finally, during a late-match offensive, Michaels put Hart in a Sharpshooter. Well before he could truly lock in the move, the referee called for the bell. Vince McMahon, who had come down to the ring midmatch, simultaneously called for the bell as well.

Michaels's music blared over the loudspeaker, as the Canadian crowd looked on in disbelief. Their hero had just lost the WWE Championship, despite never tapping out or screaming "I quit." They could tell something wasn't right.

HBK also pretended something wasn't right. He looked over to McMahon, as if to say "What's going on here?" But he knew exactly what was going on.

"Vince wanted to take 100 percent of the heat," says Michaels regarding his denying involvement. "I told him 'no way,' but he said it was his decision and he would take the heat. I understood his perspective, but in the end, I was the guy holding the gun. I was the guy who had to shoot [Bret Hart]."

After the match, Michaels, still acting as if he had no clue, grabbed his title and darted toward the back, leaving Hart in the ring alone. Mystified by what had just transpired, the former champ did the first thing that came to mind—spit a gigantic wad of phlegm directly into McMahon's face. He then signaled the letters WCW in the air with his pointer finger, before finally leaving the ring and destroying any WWE property he could get his hands on. Nothing was safe from Hart's wrath. He trashed everything from television monitors to headsets. As he continued his rampage, the Canadian crowd grew more and more enraged by the betrayal.

"It was a pretty volatile moment," recalls Hart. "I always thought

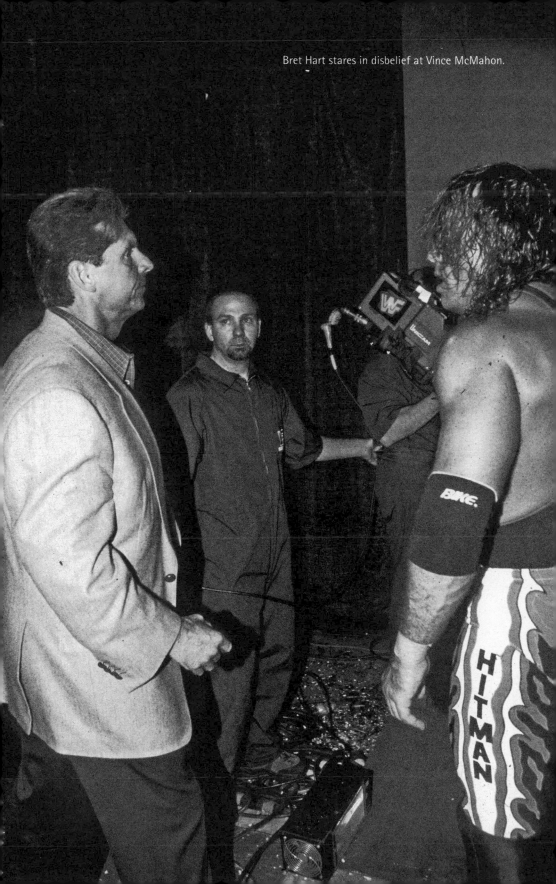

Bret Hart stares in disbelief at Vince McMahon.

that it wouldn't have taken much to start a riot in that building that night. I probably could've gotten that whole crowd to storm the back of the building and turn some cars over in the streets. It was a powder keg that night."

But the Hit Man regained his composure and headed back toward the locker room. As he walked past his puzzled family, he began to think that all his previous success had been for naught. Instead of remembering his five WWE Championship reigns, Bret Hart believed fans would now remember him for losing in Montreal.

"That was a bitter pill for me to swallow. It was a sad feeling for me to know that everything I had ever done meant so little to Vince. All my loyalty was for nothing."

Once in the back, Hart took a quick shower in an attempt to cool his mind. It didn't help. When McMahon arrived in Hart's locker room, the two engaged in a verbal altercation. After a few minutes, Hart grew tired of the words coming from his former employer's mouth, so he punched him in the face. To this day, the incident remains one of wrestling's most notorious moments, despite never being caught on camera.

"I think it was the perfect thing to do. It was fair, from my standpoint. I had been so misled and maliciously wounded in the ring. I felt so betrayed, like I had let the whole country down. I don't think people sensed how important it was for me to win that match. I still think people underestimated how proud Canada was of me at the time. So I think that dustup with Vince was the perfect response. If I had to do it all over again, I don't think I would've done anything differently. It was pretty sweet decking Vince."

McMAHON ON WWE TV, SEVEN DAYS AFTER BEING PUNCHED: I was disappointed in Bret when he hit me, very disappointed. I sustained a concussion as a result of it, with vision problems to this day. I'll get over it. I didn't think it was the right thing to do. Bret seems to be crowing about that; that I've read. He feels proud of striking me. It wasn't a question of a confrontation, because even at fifty-two years old, I dare say that perhaps things would have been a little different if there were a confrontation. I allowed Bret to strike me. I had hoped that he wouldn't. I had hoped that we could sit down and try to work things out as gentlemen. That's what I had really hoped for. But that's not what happened.

Immediately following *Survivor Series*, angered Hart fans started to point their frustration toward McMahon, claiming that "Vince screwed Bret." The WWF owner, however, saw things much differently.

McMAHON REFLECTS ON *SURVIVOR SERIES*, SEVEN DAYS LATER:

Some would say I screwed Bret Hart. Bret Hart would definitely tell you I screwed him. I look at it from a different standpoint. I look at it from the standpoint of the referee did not screw Bret Hart, Shawn Michaels certainly did not screw Bret Hart, nor did Vince McMahon screw Bret Hart. I truly believe that Bret Hart screwed Bret Hart. And he can look in the mirror and know that.

I would certainly take responsibility for any decision I ever made. I never had a problem doing that. Not that all my decisions are accurate. They're not. But when I make a bad decision, I'm not above saying "I'm sorry" and trying to do the best about it that I can. Hopefully, the batting average is pretty good. I make more good decisions than I do bad decisions. As far as screwing Bret Hart is concerned, there is a time-honored tradition in the wrestling business that when someone is leaving they show the right amount of respect to the [WWE] Superstars, in this case, who helped make you that Superstar. You show the proper respect to the organization that helped you become who you are today. It's a time-honored tradition, and Bret Hart didn't want to honor that tradition. And that's something I would've never, ever expected from Bret because he is known somewhat as a traditionalist in this business. It would've never crossed my mind that Bret would not have wanted to show the right amount of respect to the Superstars who helped make him and the organization who helped make him what he is today. Nonetheless, that was Bret's decision. Bret screwed Bret.

Who actually screwed whom is a debate that still rages today.

Michaels also found his post–*Survivor Series* life to be difficult. Many of his colleagues disagreed with his actions in Montreal, leaving HBK to fear for his safety. So he and Triple H came up with hand signals to help protect themselves.

"If something broke down, we were going to jump on whoever we had to jump on, if we could take them. If not, we were going to get the heck out of there. It was a very tense and uncomfortable time. Life got a hell of a lot harder after *Survivor Series*."

While Michaels feared for his life in WWE, Hart took his game to the rival organization. Following the events of *Survivor Series*, many believed WCW was getting sports-entertainment's hottest commodity. Unfortunately for them, though, they failed to find a way to capitalize on Hart's popularity.

HART ON HIS TIME WITH WCW: I never thought WCW and Eric Bischoff had any brains. Before I went there, I knew they were a bunch of mindless idiots who didn't know a lot about wrestling, and that I would probably sit on the bench, spin my tires, and become disgruntled. I expected all those things, and they all happened. I think Vince was the one who told me that WCW wouldn't know what to do with a Bret Hart. I remember thinking he was so right. I didn't want to leave WWE. Not for the money, not for anything. I just wanted to stay. I always thought I would go back and work for Vince after the three years with WCW.

I wanted so much to make a difference in that company. I was ready to give everything I had. And for Bischoff to say otherwise is clueless. I only did what they told me to do. There was never a case of me not wanting to do something. If anything, I tried to take their lousy ideas and make them sellable. The fact that I didn't go anywhere has to go back to them, not me.

Vince Russo was another clueless nonwrestler who never worked a match in his life. He didn't know anything about wrestling psychology or how to build a match. He had no idea. Neither did Bischoff. The average wrestling fan has more scope and psy-chology than Russo and Bischoff ever had. They were just wrestling fans.

Despite his disdain for Bischoff and Russo, the Hit Man went on to become a two-time WCW Champion. To Hart, those championship reigns couldn't compare to wearing the WWE Championship.

"Most of the time, I just threw the WCW belt in my bag and never thought twice about it. Those WCW title runs never really mattered to me. I had more important matches working for my dad. Even when I won it in Toronto, there was some stupid run-in with Dean Malenko and interference with about a half-dozen guys. It was such a convoluted ending that when I held the belt up, I almost rolled my eyes."

More than a decade after *Survivor Series*, Hart and Michaels still think back to the infamous night. Ironically, Hart is able to find some good from what happened, while HBK wishes it never happened.

HART: It's the most real thing that ever happened in wrestling, and it stands out as a pivotal moment. I think wrestlers hold me in the highest regard now as they look back and recognize that I took my responsibility as a wrestler so seriously that I had to take the posi-tion that I did. I think they respect that. I think Shawn respects that. I don't know a lot of wrestlers that would've taken the position that I did, let alone follow up afterward and knock out Vince. But it defined me as a character. It defined me as a Canadian. Years later, I got voted the thirty-ninth greatest Canadian of all time. The people who voted said they did so because I stood up to America and Vince McMahon. I'm still pretty proud of myself for that day.

MICHAELS: I regret everything with Bret. I wish I had some-thing better to say than I was angry and out of control, but I don't. I was tough to deal with back then. I felt like nobody wanted me to succeed and everybody wanted me to fail. But I was not going to let anybody take me down.

Bret had a great career and so much of it now is focused on Montreal, and that sucks. He deserves better than that. He was great at what he did, but I guess you could say that's partially his fault because he focused so much on it. It was a bad time and a bad situation.

20

ATTITUDE ERA

For years, fans presumed that Vince McMahon was nothing more than a talking head hired by WWE to describe the in-ring action each week on television. Only those close to the sports-entertainment industry actually knew of his true role as WWE owner. But as 1997 started to wind down, McMahon felt forced to pull back the curtain when he became threatened by the rising popularity of one crass Superstar. In an attempt to prevent his company's good reputation from being sullied by a single man's disrespectful antics, he finally revealed his powerful position and battled this Superstar in a very public forum. That Superstar was Stone Cold Steve Austin.

Austin arrived in WWE in January 1996 after being fired by WCW and a short stint with ECW. He debuted as the Ringmaster, Ted DiBiase's hand-picked Million Dollar Champion. As DiBiase's supposed prized pupil, Austin had little success turning fans' heads, and by midyear he had dropped the goofy "Ringmaster" moniker completely in favor of "Stone Cold."

With the new name came a new attitude. Over the next several months, the sight of Austin swilling beers and waving his middle fingers in the air became commonplace. He also developed a genuine disrespect for authority. If he was told by a WWE official to do something he objected to, he simply dropped that person with a Stone Cold Stunner.

Normally, McMahon, who began to demand he be referred to only as *Mr. McMahon*, could've simply punished Austin by preventing him from competing. But in January 1998, Stone Cold outlasted The Rock to win the *Royal Rumble*, which guaranteed him a WWE Championship Match in the main event at the biggest show of the year, *WrestleMania XIV*. This left McMahon with only one option—try to calm the beast. Unfortunately for the boss, his attempts to soothe Austin's buck-the-system attitude proved futile. Each demand McMahon made was met with either another middle finger or, worse, a Stunner.

Never before in the history of sports-entertainment had such a blatant disrespect for authority been played out in front of the television cameras, and it wasn't long before throngs of new WWE fans began to tune into *Raw* to live vicariously through the boss-beating Superstar. The innovative rivalry truly revolutionized the game and laid the foundation for what is referred to today as the Attitude Era.

"I always looked forward to Monday nights because we really seemed to have the whole world's attention," reflects Austin. "But let's be realistic about it, The Attitude Era should've been called The Stone Cold Era. I was the driving force during that period. I always took a little bit of offense to the term 'Attitude Era' because, in my mind, wrestlers should

Stone Cold Steve Austin knocks
Shawn Michaels to the floor.

always have attitude. If you don't, you're not going to be very successful. Of course, I was a different cup of tea with the select words I used and middle fingers."

With legions of new viewers behind him, Austin challenged Shawn Michaels for the WWE Championship at *WrestleMania XIV*. At the time, HBK was nearly five months into his third title reign. But despite his success, he admittedly was not in the greatest frame of mind both personally and professionally during this period of time.

"It was real difficult to work with Michaels," claims Austin. "He was like that cantankerous Ferrari: When he's ready to go, he can go like nobody else. But when he didn't want to go, there were a million reasons why he wouldn't. He did have some back problems, but he also had a lot of attitude problems and personal problems as well."

Michaels was, in fact, suffering from a back injury that eventually cost him four years of his in-ring career. He did everything in his power to conceal the severity of his condition, but there was no fooling the fans on this night. The pain on his face told the true story of a proud Superstar struggling just to stand erect. According to match commentator Jim Ross, the entire contest was a true testament to HBK's unmatched fortitude.

Despite the pain, Michaels appeared on the verge of victory. But as he went for Sweet Chin Music, Stone Cold managed to counter and connect with his patented Stunner. Special Enforcer "Iron" Mike Tyson, who assumed the role of referee after the original official was knocked out, ran into the ring and made the three count.

"Stone Cold! Stone Cold! Stone Cold!" screamed Jim Ross during his now-famous postmatch call. "The Austin Era has begun!"

Stone Cold quickly grabbed his title and began to celebrate with the raucous FleetCenter crowd in Boston. As he ascended to the second turnbuckle, he couldn't help but feel validated.

"That night, standing there with the belt in the air, for me was a giant 'screw you' to the people in WCW and Eric Bischoff, the guy who actually fired me because he didn't know what to do with me and didn't think I was marketable. I always knew I could succeed. I'll always bet on myself. I'll never forget that match, and the first time I became WWE Champion."

Ironically, the match's loser, HBK, also found reason to celebrate.

"Losing that match was such a relief. It was the best for me and the company. I would have exploded otherwise," claims Michaels, regarding the physical and mental stresses he was under. "From that point on, the company enjoyed tremendous success. And so did I."

Keep your friends close and your enemies closer. At least that's what Mr. McMahon was thinking following *WrestleMania*. Fearing an uncontrolled Stone Cold reign would result in a public relations nightmare for WWE, McMahon actually tried to join forces with the new champ. The owner claimed that with his business prowess and Austin's physical talent, Stone Cold would become the greatest WWE Champion of all time. In reality, McMahon was simply trying to get closer to Austin so he could control his behavior.

Austin instantly spotted McMahon's insincerity, and rather than join forces with the scheming boss, he dropped him with a Stunner. The assault finally opened McMahon's eyes to the fact that he was never going to change the Texas Rattlesnake. So he had his champ arrested and began to plot Plan C.

Mr. McMahon combed his roster, looking for the perfect Superstar to take down Austin. He needed a man with superior in-ring ability and just enough naiveté to not realize he was being taken advantage of by the boss. McMahon chose Dude Love, one of Mick Foley's many alter egos.

Over the next several months, McMahon stacked the deck heavily in Dude Love's favor. But Austin managed to overcome the odds each time to retain the title, including matches at *Unforgiven* and *Over the Edge*. Realizing he was getting nowhere fast, McMahon traded Dude Love for Kane and declared a First Blood Match between Stone Cold and the "Big Red Machine" at *King of the Ring*. During this time period, Kane was covered from head to toe in ring gear, including a thick mask that covered his face. This made Austin's job considerably harder.

Further exasperating the issue for Stone Cold was his rough road to *King of the Ring,* one that was paved with an unexpected stay in the hospital.

"I wrestled Mick Foley in the Houston Summit several days before *King of the Ring*," remembers Austin. "After the match, I couldn't stop shivering. I had a hundred-and-four-degree fever. It turned out I had a staph infection in my elbow. So I was in the hospital for five days, hooked up to IVs and getting the infection fixed. When I finally got out of my hospital bed, I had to go to *King of the Ring* and go up against a physical specimen like Kane with my arm all taped up. It was difficult."

But he did it. From the beginning of the match, it was clear that Austin's game plan was to keep the action inside the ring and away from the numerous metal objects traditionally found on the outside. The plan worked well early on, but when the Hell in a Cell cage that was used earlier in the evening began to mysteriously make its way back down to the ring, things began to look bleak for the champ. Hoping to draw blood, Kane repeatedly rammed the champ's skull into the steel. Miraculously, though, Austin failed to shed an ounce of blood.

Watching from the back, Mankind, who had failed to defeat Austin at the prior two Pay-Per-Views (as Dude Love), decided to take matters into his own hands. Armed with a steel chair, Foley made his way toward the ring with ill intentions. Little did he know, though, he was not alone. Following closely behind him was a chair-wielding Undertaker. Once the Deadman hit the ring, he cocked his chair and swung it at Foley; but his target ducked, resulting in Stone Cold becoming the unintentional recipient. The impact of the blow created a bloody gash on Austin's head. Crimson streamed down his face, and the referee called for the bell. Stone Cold's red-hot reign had come to a shocking end.

Instead of wallowing in the loss, Austin set his sights on getting back what he rightfully thought was his, and just twenty-four hours after *King of the Ring*, toppled Kane on *Raw* to reclaim the WWE Championship. The victory infuriated Mr. McMahon, who thought he had finally foiled his rival. Unfortunately for him, though, he failed; and this time, Austin planned on being even more rebellious, starting with trashing the traditional WWE Championship in favor of a more attitudinal version known as the Smoking Skull Belt.

"I have to give credit for that idea to the Road Warriors, Mike and Joe (Hawk and Animal)," admits Austin. "They came up to me and said somebody like Stone Cold should have his own belt. I think it really tied in with the attitude of my championship runs. And damn, we sold millions of those damn things."

Austin's second reign picked up where his first left off. Over the next three months, he continued to succeed in the ring and draw huge ratings, all the while infuriating his boss. Finally in September 1998, with hopes of destroying Stone Cold once and for all, McMahon assembled sports-entertainment's most awesome force: Undertaker *and* Kane.

The pairing proved to be a stroke of genius, as the destructive duo was able to take the title from Austin in a Triple Threat Match at *Breakdown*, but not without controversy. In the contest's closing seconds, Undertaker and Kane hit Stone Cold with a double chokeslam. Both then proceeded to cover the champ, while the referee counted to three. The bell rang, signifying the end of Austin's reign, but because both Superstars had made the cover, it wasn't clear which had won.

Several seconds went by without an official word. Finally, ring announcer Howard Finkel began to speak.

"The winner of this bout and *new* World Wrestling Federation Champion . . ."

Silence.

Much like in the 1994 *Royal Rumble*, Finkel didn't know how to finish the sentence: Was it Undertaker or Kane?

Tired of the confusion, Mr. McMahon marched to the ring, grabbed the title, and stormed off. The following night on *Raw*, a proud McMahon stood in the ring prepared to present the gold to either Undertaker or Kane. But before he could officially name a new champion, Austin charged through the arena on a Zamboni, knocking over thousands of dollars of production equipment in the process. Once he hit the ring, the former champ dove from the Zamboni's hood directly onto Mr. McMahon. The interruption effectively ended the title presentation ceremony and also sent Stone Cold straight to jail.

Putting Austin in the slammer wasn't enough for McMahon. The evil owner also wished to humiliate his nemesis like never before. To accomplish this, he forced Stone Cold to officiate a WWE Championship Match between Undertaker and Kane at *Judgment Day*. At the end of the contest, Austin would have no choice but to present what he believed was his title to the winner. To ensure the former champ would go through with the humbling act, McMahon guaranteed he would fire Stone Cold if he failed to do as he was told.

When *Judgment Day* rolled into the Rosemont Horizon on October 18, 1998, many fans assumed Austin wouldn't show. They thought he had too much dignity to present another Superstar with his title. Those fans were wrong . . . partially. Stone Cold did in fact show up to officiate the match that night. But his idea of being a referee was a bit different than the norm. After Undertaker smacked Kane with a steel chair, Austin took it upon himself to also get involved in the action. He gave Undertaker a Stunner, followed by a chair shot to the head. With both Undertaker and Kane down on the mat, Stone Cold dropped to his knees and counted all four shoulders down.

After the bell rang, Austin got on the microphone and announced himself as the winner of the match. It wasn't at all what McMahon had hoped for when he devised his devious plan. Irate, he screamed at Austin from a secure box behind the TitanTron. But it was nearly impossible to hear a single word over the chants of "A-hole!" from the Rosemont crowd.

They eventually quieted long enough for the boss to get his message out. "Stone Cold, screw you, you're fired!"

Overnight, thousands of fans sent letters of protest to WWE headquarters in Stamford, Connecticut. Their message was simple: If there was no Steve Austin in WWE, they would not watch. Luckily for them, Stone Cold wouldn't be gone for long. Mr. McMahon's son, Shane McMahon, inked Austin to a new multiyear deal shortly after *Judgment Day*.

21

THE CORPORATE CHAMP

Love him or hate him, Mr. McMahon has to be respected for

his ability to read the WWE fans. After *Judgment Day* failed

to crown a new titlist, he sensed the audience was growing

weary of the instability surrounding the WWE Championship.

So to satisfy his loyal viewers, the owner and CEO made one

of his famous guarantees, claiming that there would be a new champ crowned at the next Pay-Per-View, *Survivor Series*.

To fill the void at the top of his roster, McMahon announced a fourteen-man single elimination tournament, similar to the one held at *WrestleMania IV* ten years prior. Earning entry into the tournament were Goldust, Ken Shamrock, Big Boss Man, The Rock, Steve Austin, Triple H, Steven Regal, X-Pac, Jeff Jarrett, Al Snow, Mankind, Undertaker, and Kane. A mystery newcomer was also booked for the event. But Mr. McMahon vowed to keep his identity under wraps until the start of the Pay-Per-View.

In the weeks leading up to *Survivor Series*, McMahon's list of enemies increased in number. The most notable names joining Stone Cold were his own son, Shane McMahon, and The Rock. Vince fired Shane in the wake of his questionable contract negotiations with Austin. He then quickly rehired him, but only to serve as a lowly referee. Mr. McMahon's problems with The Rock were a bit more superficial. At the time, The Rock was promoting himself as the "People's Champion," and because McMahon had a problem with the "people," he also had a problem with their champion.

Around the same time, Mankind began to develop a deep fondness for McMahon. The formerly deranged Superstar had softened considerably and now made it his chief responsibility to be there for McMahon, whether the boss needed some protection or even a good laugh. Mr. McMahon appeared annoyed by Mankind's undying affection, but he never let the peculiar Superstar know his true feelings. Instead, he kept Mankind close, using him as a pawn in his ultimate plan that would unfold at *Survivor Series*.

When *Survivor Series* aired on Sunday, November 15, 1998, Jim Ross announced that the tournament's brackets had been hand-selected by Mr. McMahon. To the unsuspecting viewer, these appeared to make The Rock's route to the finals nearly impossible. On the flip side, Mankind's bracket was manipulated in such a fashion that a trip to the finals was almost guaranteed, especially after his first-round mystery opponent was revealed.

Reading from a prepared statement, McMahon gushed over his newest acquisition, calling the mysterious Superstar a "legend in the ranks of sports-entertainment," among many other flattering descriptions. It was none other than Duane Gill, an unknown Superstar with thousands of losses attached to his résumé.

At that moment, it became clear that McMahon's description of Gill dripped with sarcasm. It also appeared that the boss was making Mankind's trip to the finals even easier than it originally appeared. A mere thirty seconds later, Gill had racked up yet another loss and Mankind was on his way to the quarterfinals, without even breaking a sweat. As the tournament raged on, Mankind continued to advance with the greatest of ease. His only true competition was Stone Cold, but he quickly cleared that hurdle when referee Shane McMahon screwed Austin out of advancing. Up until that point, both Stone Cold and the fans assumed Shane could be trusted. Clearly, this was not the case; he was in his father's camp all along.

On the surface, The Rock's road to the finals looked daunting. But he managed to get there thanks to a series of supposed miscues by McMahon's men, most notably Big Boss Man, who lost to the Brahma Bull in less than five seconds.

When it all shook out, the finals featured McMahon's hand-picked Superstar, Mankind, against heavy fan favorite The Rock. During the match, referee Earl Hebner conveniently looked the other way while Mankind took several liberties with the rules, including the use of a chair and biting his opponent's face.

"The Mankind era in [WWE] is about to dawn!" screamed Jim Ross, as The Rock began to fade from the Mandible Claw. But the People's Champ somehow retained consciousness. After several minutes of being caught in Mankind's clutches, he finally broke free and hit his patented Rock Bottom. Uncharacteristically, The Rock then locked Mankind's legs into a Sharpshooter. The hold wasn't applied for very long before McMahon, who was stationed ringside, called for the bell and awarded the match to The Rock. Something wasn't right. The moment was eerily similar to the closing moments of the previous year's *Survivor Series*, where Bret Hart also lost the WWE Championship despite never submitting to the Sharpshooter.

Shane McMahon climbed into the ring and raised The Rock's hand in victory, cementing the fans' fearful suspicions that their hero was in collusion with the McMahons all along. For the second *Survivor Series* in a row, the crowd was scorned by the boss. Mr. McMahon, however, saw things differently.

"Vince McMahon didn't screw the people tonight," he said while

Vince and Shane McMahon honor the crowning of The Rock as champ.

being showered with boos. "The people screwed the people. And you can all believe that each and every one of you are just as pathetic and gullible as Mankind."

Mankind struggled to comprehend what had just happened. To him, McMahon was a close confidant; in reality, however, he was simply being used to ensure The Rock would become WWE Champion.

Before *Survivor Series* went off the air, the younger McMahon grabbed the microphone to put the exclamation point on the evening. "The McMahon family is proud to present your new [WWE] Champion, the Corporate Champion. I give you, The Rock."

Mr. McMahon finally had the Corporate Champion he long desired. And to ensure his man maintained a firm grasp of the gold, the boss continually added new pieces to his faction, including Ken Shamrock, Kane, and then-commissioner Shawn Michaels. But the growing Corporation did little to deter Mankind, who was determined to get revenge.

Mankind appeared to accomplish his goal at *Rock Bottom* when he forced the Brahma Bull to pass out due to the Mandible Claw. But before the challenger could be awarded the title, Mr. McMahon declared that The Rock would retain the gold, stating the champion never actually tapped out. The shady decision was heart wrenching for Mankind, who had fought the fight of his life only to walk away with nothing.

Following the soul-crushing events at *Rock Bottom*, it became clear to Mankind that he would need more than just a great in-ring performance to wrest the title away from The Rock. So he enlisted D-Generation X to be at his side for the *Raw* rematch.

The normally rebellious faction did what they could to ensure justice, but not even DX could stop McMahon's men from intruding in the match. The Corporation's interference didn't go unnoticed by Austin, who was watching from the back. Determined to spoil the night for his longtime rival, Mr. McMahon, Stone Cold charged the ring and clobbered The Rock with a steel chair. He then dragged Mankind over Rock's fallen body, and the referee counted to three.

Mankind had done the unthinkable. He had captured the WWE Championship and brought down McMahon's powerful Corporation, albeit with some help from DX and Austin. The crazed and comical Superstar dedicated the win to his "two little people at home," then celebrated with a few victory laps around the ring.

Mankind's championship win came at a very pivotal time in the Monday Night Wars. By this time, WWE had finally regained the momentum in the *Raw-Nitro* ratings battle. Feeling the heat, WCW had scheduled a mega main event between Hulk Hogan and Kevin Nash to go up against the Mankind–Rock match. WCW was convinced they had the star power to win the night's ratings, but just to be sure, Eric Bischoff ordered *Nitro* commentator Tony Schiavone to reveal the results of the prerecorded Mankind-Rock match before it ever aired. The decision proved to be a cardinal mistake. Realizing history was being made on *Raw*, millions of viewers abandoned the live *Nitro* to watch the lovable Mankind win the gold. WCW never recovered. They spent the next two years playing second fiddle to WWE, before finally waving the white flag in March 2001.

The Rock's rematch came in the form of an "I Quit" Match at the 1999 *Royal Rumble*. On paper, the contest heavily favored Mankind, who, over the course of his career, had willingly battled through barbed wire, thumbtacks, beds of nails, and countless other life-threatening weapons without ever once uttering the words "I quit."

Heading into the event, The Rock displayed an undying determination to change history. He threatened Mankind with a countless series of Rock Bottoms and People's Elbows. Inside, though, he knew he would need so much more than a sideslam and silly elbow drop to stop Mankind. So he devised a plan that combined never-before-seen brutality with a little treachery.

More than a decade later, the encounter is still regarded as *the* most vicious WWE Championship Match of all time. The first half of the contest saw The Rock whack Mankind with whatever wasn't nailed down, including ladders and the steel ringside steps. The action eventually escalated to the top of the *Royal Rumble* entryway, where The Rock did the unthinkable and tossed his opponent down onto a set of live electrical circuits. Sparks of electricity shot from the unit, causing Shane McMahon to run from the back and beg The Rock to stop. But the resolute challenger ignored his ally's request and dragged Mankind back into the ring, where he handcuffed his hands behind his back.

With Mankind unable to defend himself, The Rock proceeded to crush the champ's skull with an unprecedented number of shots from a steel chair. The 15,000 fans in Arrowhead Pond cringed with each passing blow. Many fans screamed for the match to be stopped, while others left altogether, including Mankind's wife and two sobbing children, who had front-row seats for the carnage.

The protests failed to stop The Rock, who kept punishing Mankind with shot after shot. After a while, the champ started to slowly make his way up the aisle toward the back. It's uncertain if he was disoriented or simply trying to dodge The Rock's inexorable attack. Either way, it didn't matter: The Rock was right behind him the whole way, striking the champ with the cold steel.

Finally, the challenger took a few steps back. Some thought he might finally be relenting. In reality, he was getting a running start for his final home-run swing. *Whack!* The Rock connected yet again. The challenger then grabbed the microphone and placed it in front of the champ's prone body.

"I quit, I quit, I quit," shouted Mankind.

The Rock had done the impossible. He had finally forced the deranged Mankind to scream the fateful phrase that nobody ever thought he would say. Or did he? It was later learned that Mankind never actually said "I quit" that night. Instead, The Rock had slyly piped in a recording from an earlier interview where Mankind said the words. By the time anybody realized what had happened, it was too late. The Rock had already been awarded his second WWE Championship.

"The way I see it, there's going to be an awful lot of bored people during halftime of the big game," said Mankind to The Rock, one day after losing the WWE Championship. The prophetic words were not just a dig at Big Bad Voodoo Daddy, Gloria Estefan, and Stevie Wonder, who were scheduled to perform during the halftime show of Super Bowl XXXIII; they were also the makings of a truly unique challenge. In an attempt to give football fans something worth watching, Mankind suggested to The Rock that they

square off on a special edition of *WWE Sunday Night Heat* that would air during halftime of the big game. The new champ accepted, setting the stage for the latest chapter in the Mankind-Rock saga.

Unlike their prior battles, which were littered with passionate fans, not a single person witnessed The Rock defend against Mankind live. Instead, the championship rematch took place in WWE's first-ever Empty Arena Match. Never before had the WWE title been on the line in such an unorthodox fashion, but while the atmosphere was certainly unique, the brutality of the contest managed to mimic their past matches.

Realizing they had the entire arena to themselves, The Rock and Mankind only battled inside the ring during the match's earliest moments. The action almost immediately spilled out into the empty seats, where the champ buried his challenger under a mound of steel folding chairs. From there, the dueling Superstars covered nearly every inch of the arena, including the upper deck, kitchen, and corporate offices. They even took the fight outside into the loading-dock area. The fresh air effectively revitalized Mankind, who was stuck on the defensive for the majority of the match. Once outside, he applied his paralyzing Mandible Claw to the champ. The hold rendered The Rock unconscious long enough for Mankind to drape a pallet of six beer kegs across his opponent's chest using a forklift. Unable to break free from the crushing weight of six kegs, The Rock had no choice but to lie there helplessly while Mankind scored the pinfall. A mere seven days after losing the title at the *Royal Rumble*, Mankind was once again on top of the wrestling world.

The epic Mankind-Rock rivalry continued through mid-February, when the two rivals competed in a Ladder Match on *Raw*. Despite having only hours of WWE experience, Big Show (known then as Paul Wight) played a major role in the outcome of the contest. The giant newcomer had just come over from rival WCW, where he had enjoyed two reigns as their champion. That past success, however, was all washed away the moment he set foot into a WWE locker room. And although he stands an unbelievable seven feet tall, Big Show admits to feeling a bit nervous that first time: "I was a young kid at the time, a new star, so to speak. It was very intimidating. I couldn't believe how intense these guys were. It was completely different from where I was. In WCW, if you had a hangnail, you took two weeks off. In WWE,

Undertaker would work with a hundred-and-three fever and dysentery, for crying out loud. And he'd still tear the house down. It was unlike anything else I had ever experienced."

After seeing Mankind slip Mr. Socko into the mouth of The Rock during the Ladder Match, Big Show swallowed his nerves and purposefully walked to the ring, where he grabbed the champ by the throat and chokeslammed him nearly through the mat. The assist allowed Show's Corporation cohort, The Rock, to scale the ladder and capture the gold.

The win not only gave the Brahma Bull his third WWE Championship, it also marked the conclusion of one of the most vicious rivalries ever. In the weeks that followed, Mankind shifted his focus toward exacting revenge from Big Show, while The Rock prepared for *WrestleMania XV* and Stone Cold Steve Austin.

22

STONE COLD
VERSUS THE ROCK

Ask any WWE Superstar what it takes to be a great cham-

pion and almost all of them will tell you that charisma plays

a major role. Over the course of the nearly fifty-year his-

tory of the WWE Championship, many of the most legendary

titlists have backed up this theory with their quick wit and motivational microphone skills: "Superstar" Billy Graham, Hulk Hogan, Ric Flair, Shawn Michaels. But while all were certainly entertaining in their own way, they all take a backseat to The Rock and Stone Cold Steve Austin.

After The Rock finally moved past his war with Mankind, the WWE Champion found himself on a collision course with Stone Cold. The result— one of the most entertaining and charismatic rivalries to ever grace a WWE ring.

From the moment The Rock entered WWE, it was clear he was dripping with personality. Not once did he ever show a sliver of trepidation when speaking to a sold-out crowd. Stone Cold displayed the same level of confidence . . . but his excellence was not second nature.

"When I look back at my promos from World Class Championship Wrestling and the few I did as 'Stunning' Steve Austin (in WCW), I pretty much blew. But goddamn, they were real. They weren't scripted. That forced me to learn my A-game. There are very few people who just start out with an A-game—I wasn't one of them.

"I remember when they put me and Brian Pillman together as the Hollywood Blondes [in 1993]. Pillman was always a really good talker. We used to ride down the road together, and I'd look over and there's Pillman reading a vocabulary book. He was always working on getting better. That's when I thought, 'If this guy is going to go this far, I better bring myself up to speed.' Then I went to ECW and got some more opportunity and learned even more."

By the time he reached WWE, more specifically his rivalry with The Rock, Austin was a star showman. His catchphrases, such as "That's the bottom line 'cause Stone Cold said so" and "Austin 3:16 says I just whipped your ass," were consistently repeated by fans all over the globe. And it wasn't just the spoken word that made him so popular—it was also his actions, particularly his beer drinking and bird flipping. Fans simply loved the working-class hero who wasn't afraid to be a little edgy.

As the rivalry neared *WrestleMania XV*, Austin's edginess reached a whole new level when he drove a monster beer truck into an arena and soaked down The Rock, Shane, and Mr. McMahon. The sight of Stone Cold operating the giant beer hose is still used on WWE highlight reels today. But what many don't realize is that it didn't go quite as planned for Austin.

Stone Cold Steve Austin vs. The Rock.

"When they hit me with that idea, I said, 'damn, that's badass,' " recalls Austin. "But what they didn't see on camera was me trying to give myself a drink. The only problem was that I forgot to take my thumb off the nozzle, causing all this beer to come shooting at me. If I had tonsils, it would've washed them right down my throat. But we were live, and when that red light's on, I'm always going to regain my composure very quickly. So I acted like nothing happened, but damn, it turned my eyelids inside out. But the funniest part was watching Vince do that crazy swim thing he did."

While Austin appeared to be having a good time on camera, in reality, a bitter divorce was causing mountains of stress in his personal life. Recognizing the pressure was mounting, WWE arranged for Stone Cold to be flown to Philadelphia, the site of *WrestleMania XV*, on a private jet. The gesture helped relieve him of some anxiety, but it failed to fully clear his head while he was packing for the trip.

"I was going through so much at that time. Man, I even forgot to pack my [signature] vest. Here it is, the biggest night of the year, and I don't have my vest. I had to walk to the ring with a T-shirt on."

Once March 28, 1999, came, Stone Cold put his personal issues on hold and focused solely on his *WrestleMania* match with The Rock. Both Superstars took full advantage of the no-disqualification stipulation and battled much of the match outside the ring, utilizing various weapons found around the arena, including the enormous *WrestleMania XV* sign that hung above the entryway. In the end, Austin nailed The Rock with a Stunner, causing the champ to bounce around the ring like a pinball. Once he finally settled, Stone Cold went for the pin and the win.

To the outsider, Austin's celebration looked much like his *WrestleMania XIV* postmatch bash. Inside, though, the feeling couldn't have been any different.

"It was a tough night at the office," says Austin. "I remember it being such a tremendous relief when we got the three count in and the bell rang. At the time, Coors Light was on tap, and they threw me a couple of those silver cans and when I clicked those damn things together and stood up on that turnbuckle, I remember thinking to myself 'I made it,' meaning I made it through the match that I was so stressed about, in spite of all the distractions going on in my personal life."

• • •

Stone Cold defeated the Brahma Bull again at the following month's *Back-lash* Pay-Per-View. The win temporarily ended the Austin-Rock rivalry, but the real story of the night happened just moments after his victory. As the show reached its conclusion, an innocent Stephanie McMahon was seen in the back of a limousine, preparing to leave for the night. Before the car left, however, the evil Undertaker revealed himself as the driver. He locked Stephanie inside the vehicle and sped off.

The next night on *Raw,* the Deadman's Ministry of Darkness carried a restrained Stephanie to the ring on an oversized Undertaker symbol. According to the Deadman, if Mr. McMahon failed to give him ownership of WWE, the Phenom was going to perform a black wedding ceremony, uniting himself and the boss's daughter forever. Both Ken Shamrock and Big Show tried to stop the dark plan, but neither could penetrate the Ministry's defenses. Finally, just moments before the ceremony was to be completed, the most unlikely of heroes ran to the ring to save the day: Stone Cold Steve Austin.

The champ cleared house of the Undertaker's henchmen before finally untying Stephanie, who showed her appreciation by wrapping her arms around Austin and giving him an emotional embrace. Fans couldn't believe their eyes; Stone Cold had just saved his archrival's daughter. But he didn't do it for Mr. McMahon; he did it because it was the right thing to do.

Unfortunately for Austin, his heroism was rewarded with a title defense against Undertaker at *Over the Edge.* Marred by controversial officiating by special guest referee Shane McMahon, the match concluded with the Deadman ending Stone Cold's third WWE Championship reign with a simple rollup.

23

IT'S ALL ABOUT THE GAME

Stone Cold Steve Austin went on to regain the WWE Championship from Undertaker in June 1999, only to turn around and lose it to Mankind two months later. For Mankind, it was his third WWE Championship reign. It was also his shortest. Just one night after winning the gold, the Deranged One would serve as the launching pad for one of the most historic championship careers of all time.

As cofounder and eventual leader of D-Generation X, Triple H became one of the most popular Superstars of the late 1990s. But despite all the fanfare, The Game knew that leading the rebellious faction could only get him so far. So in March 1999, he turned on DX to join forces with Mr. McMahon's corrupt Corporation. Aligning himself with the boss caused Triple H to lose legions of fans, but to him, they were simply collateral damage in a war for championship status.

Sans X-Pac and the New Age Outlaws, The Game spent the next several months atop the card, vying for the WWE title. Each time, though, he fell just short of his ultimate goal. Sensing his August opportunity on *Raw* could be his last, Triple H, behind the stroke of the powerful Corporation, concocted a foolproof plan that would finally put the gold around his waist.

After Mankind refused to put his newly won title on the line against The Game, Shane McMahon used his power to demand the champ defend against Triple H on *Raw*. Furthermore, Shane appointed himself as the match's referee.

With that, not only did The Game get his chance at the gold, but he also became the odds-on-favorite to win. As expected, Shane failed to call the action down the middle. He even went so far as to blatantly ignore pin attempts by Mankind. After several minutes of wildly shoddy officiating, Triple H finally put Mankind's one-day reign out of its misery after flattening the champ with a Pedigree.

The Game's victory quenched a near five-year thirst for WWE's ultimate prize. Since joining WWE in 1995, he experienced many professional ups and downs, including an extended stay in Vince McMahon's doghouse for breaking unwritten rules of conduct. But he refused to give up, and on August 23, 1999, he finally captured the first of what would be a record-setting number of WWE Championships.

But with newfound success came a new obsession. Simply being the best in the industry wasn't enough for Triple H. He also wanted to prove that he was the most powerful man in all of WWE . . . even more powerful than the McMahons. To help demonstrate this supposed supremacy, he set out on a series of verbal attacks pointed at Vince and his wife, Linda. In

the beginning, Vince let The Game's barbs roll off his back, but when the champ started making sexual innuendos toward Linda, the protective husband had no choice but to fight.

In retrospect, Triple H would admit that going after the boss was not the wisest idea. Despite punishing McMahon for much of their match, The Game was ultimately dethroned when Stone Cold interfered, dropping the champ with a Stunner. From there, guest referee Shane—the same man who had helped Triple H win the gold three weeks prior—made the historic three count and awarded the WWE Championship to his father. In an ironic twist, The Game would later go on to marry the owner's daughter, Stephanie, making Triple H and Vince the only father–son-in-law combination to hold the WWE title.

While embarrassing, the loss to Mr. McMahon did little to slow down the Cerebral Assassin. After the WWE owner willingly vacated the title on September 20, 1999, Triple H quickly snatched it back up when he outlasted Big Show, the British Bulldog, The Rock, Kane, and Mankind in a Six-Pack Challenge at *Unforgiven* later that month.

Triple H was originally scheduled to defend his WWE Championship against Stone Cold and The Rock at the 1999 *Survivor Series*. Prior to the event, however, Austin was brutally run down in a vehicular assault outside the arena. The attack sidelined the Texas Rattlesnake for nine months, but more immediately, it left a gaping hole in the upcoming Triple Threat Match, a hole that would ultimately be filled by the enormous Big Show.

The last-minute inclusion of Big Show certainly shocked Triple H and The Rock, who struggled to find a way to offset their opponent's massive size advantage. After several failed attempts to chop the giant down individually, they eventually teamed up to send Show crashing through the table of the Spanish announcers. But the attack only took the big man out of the picture temporarily. He eventually worked his way back into the ring, where he chokeslammed Triple H and pinned him to capture the title. The shocking victory gave Big Show the honor of being just the sixth man in history to win both the WWE and NWA/WCW Championships. Buddy Rogers, Ric Flair, Hulk Hogan, Randy Savage, and Kevin Nash were the others.

"To be honest, I don't know if that reign was a direct compliment

to my skills in the ring as a leader or even a good champion," admits Big Show today. "I think it was just dumb luck. I was in the right place at the right time. I'm not trying to be humble, but when you look at the WWE Champions of that era, you see Bret Hart, Shawn Michaels, Stone Cold Steve Austin, The Rock, Triple H . . . These guys deserved to be champions. With me, though, it was really just luck."

Whether he deserved it or not, Big Show was the top man, and he was quickly learning that being the WWE Champion was far different than holding the WCW title. When he was representing the rival, he admits to never feeling stressed or pressured. Instead, Show likened his time on top of WCW to a fan getting to hang out with his favorite wrestlers. Despite never actually having to learn how to wrestle, he was able to roll with the likes of Hulk Hogan and Ric Flair.

"My bosses didn't demand my best, and they didn't give their best in return," recalls Show. "That's the thing about Vince McMahon. He might be an asshole at times, but the one thing I respect is that he made me a better Superstar and person. He goes out and gives one-hundred-and-ten percent and he expects the same from us. I know he gets angry when people put him over, but I really respect him as a business person. A lot of the attitude I used to have, I totally changed after working with him for ten years."

Big Boss Man emerged as the first Superstar to come gunning for Big Show's gold in December 1999. Their rivalry was filled with personal animosity—Boss Man crashed the funeral of Big Show's father, dragging the coffin around the cemetery from the back of his car—but because neither Superstar was the card's best competitor, their *Armageddon* match failed to be given main event status. Instead, the honors went to Mr. McMahon and Triple H.

"That's the thing: Champion or not, the best match is going to be the main event," says Show. "Vince and Triple H was a very hot angle at the time. And Triple H could have a match with a broomstick and make it look good. Wrestling Vince is like wrestling a *muscled up* broomstick. As knowledgeable and creative as he is, he is absolutely the most unathletic person I've ever seen in the ring. He's like a hand grenade in the back of a cement truck. Regardless, that was the match of the night, and it deserved to be the main event."

Moments before the night's main event, Big Show made quick work of Boss Man, defeating him with a chokeslam after just three minutes. With the win, the oversized champion was able to carry the title into 2000. Unfortunately for him, however, he didn't get very far. Only three days in, he was picked off by Triple H on *Raw*.

"The hardest part of losing the championship is when you pack your bags the next couple of days and you feel like you're missing something," says Show. "That's hard to get used to. But the fact that it was Triple H made it a little easier. He's probably my oldest friend in the business. I actually started with him years ago back in the WCW Power Plant. Triple H is one of the guys who gave me my chokeslam."

A lot changed between Triple H's first and third WWE Championship victories. Not only had he reconciled with D-Generation X, but he had also married Stephanie McMahon, which finally gave him the ultimate power he so deeply desired. During what became known as the McMahon-Helmsley Era, Triple H and Stephanie recklessly ruled WWE, making questionable decisions at the expense of their fellow Superstars.

Their chief target was Mick Foley.

Intoxicated by power, the couple inexplicably fired Foley in late 1999, only to hire him back early the following year. The quizzical administration decisions eventually led to a series of grueling championship matches between the two Superstars, starting with a Street Fight at the 2000 *Royal Rumble*.

The dangerous Street Fight environment heavily favored Foley, who competed in the match under his legendary hardcore persona, Cactus Jack. As Cactus, Foley was able to slip into a psychotic state in which personal pain was considered a delicacy. It wasn't uncommon to see him battle on beds of nails, shards of glass, or even C-4 explosives, all while displaying his famous toothless grin.

Stephanie escorted Triple H to the ring but refused to stay for the carnage. Prior to the opening bell, she gave her husband a kiss before walking to the back, knowing full well that her man would never be the same again.

Once the match started, the action proved to be even more intense than anticipated. Both Superstars quickly moved past the traditional use of steel chairs and ring steps en route to a more vicious bag of tricks. The sold-out Madison Square Garden gasped as The Game slammed Cactus with a barbed-wire-covered two-by-four. But the attack failed to stop the challenger, who had been victimized by similar weapons countless times in the past. In fact Cactus was able to grab the two-by-four and turn it around on Triple H.

The brutality went on to include handcuffs and the announcers' table, among other items, but it was the smallest weapon of all that proved most effective. Late in the contest, Cactus pulled a bag of tiny thumbtacks from under the ring and scattered them all over the mat. He tried to drive the champ into the piercing objects but was instead backflipped into them himself. Thousands of thumbtacks punctured Cactus's body. He slowly worked his way back up to his feet but was quickly greeted by two match-ending Pedigrees on top of the tacks.

Despite coming up short in the career-altering Street Fight, Cactus continued to be a thorn in Triple H's side after the *Royal Rumble*, leaving the champ no choice but to offer the persistent challenger a rematch. This time, the contest would take place inside Hell in a Cell. Furthermore, Foley's career was on the line.

Amazingly, the Hell in a Cell's brutality managed to surpass that of

Triple H vs. The Rock.

Victory for The Rock.

the Street Fight. Toward the end of the match, with both Superstars standing atop the steel structure, Cactus nailed The Game with a flaming two-
by-four covered in barbed wire. He then went for a Piledriver, but the
champ had the move well scouted and backflipped the challenger instead.
The force of the flip sent Cactus crashing through the Cell's roof, as well as
the ring below. Triple H added a Pedigree for good measure before finally
putting the finishing touches on Foley's career.

In November 1998, The Rock used his alliance with Mr. McMahon to
springboard himself to the WWE Championship. Fifteen months later, the
Brahma Bull hoped that same alliance would bring him to the promised
land yet again. With the WWE boss in his corner, The Rock challenged
Triple H for the gold at *WrestleMania 2000* in a Fatal Four Way elimination match that also featured Big Show and a returning Foley.

The Rock's chances of regaining the gold greatly increased following
early exits by Big Show and Foley. But just when it looked like the People's
Champ had the title within his reach, Mr. McMahon showed his true colors

by whacking The Rock with a steel chair. The double cross helped Triple H pick up the win, making him only the third WWE Champion to successfully retain his title over the course of *WrestleMania*'s sixteen-year history (Hulk Hogan and Diesel were the others).

By helping his son-in-law win at *WrestleMania*, Mr. McMahon was able to smooth his oft-rocky relationship with daughter Stephanie and son Shane. The only McMahon who wasn't wild about the betrayal was Linda, who sympathized with The Rock by putting Stone Cold in his corner for his upcoming *Backlash* title opportunity against Triple H. The authoritative decision helped offset the enormous numbers advantage of The Game, who had both Stephanie and Mr. McMahon in his corner, as well as Shane serving as special guest referee.

Even with the Rattlesnake in his corner, the odds appeared simply too insurmountable for The Rock. Realizing this, Linda made a shrewd move late in the match that helped swing the momentum back in the challenger's favor. With Shane still feeling the effects of an earlier Rock Bottom, Linda walked to the ring with her own unbiased referee. The Rock then hit the champ with a spinebuster, followed by the People's Elbow, and went for the cover. Seeing the end of her son-in-law's dishonorable reign in sight, Linda demanded her ref to make the three count.

The Rock's fourth WWE Championship reign was much like his previous three—short. Less than one month in, he lost the title back to Triple H in a grueling sixty-minute WWE Iron Man Match at *Judgment Day*. Luckily for The Rock, he was able to regain the gold from The Game just one month later at *King of the Ring*. The victory capped off a wild rivalry that saw The Rock and Triple H trade the title three times over the course of just two months.

24

WCW'S FINAL DAYS

Very few Superstars are able to reach sports-entertainment's pinnacle their rookie year. Traditionally, a competitor spends years, sometimes decades, honing his craft before even being considered worthy of a WWE Championship Match. Randy Savage wrestled for fifteen years before claiming his first title. Bret Hart bounced around for sixteen years prior to his number being called. And Sgt. Slaughter had to wait an amazing twenty years before finally wrapping the gold around his waist.

All of these men were great athletes, but then again, none were Kurt Angle.

Armed with an extensive amateur wrestling background that included a 1996 Olympic gold medal, Angle was able to hit the ground running upon making his WWE debut in November 1999. Within months, he had added the European and Intercontinental Championships to his trophy case. He also defeated Rikishi to win the prestigious *King of the Ring* tournament in June 2000. Even the most casual fan could recognize that they were witnessing the start of something special.

Angle's road to immortality would have to go through The Rock, whom he challenged for the WWE Championship at *No Mercy*. In the weeks leading up to the event, Rikishi revealed that he was the one driving the car that struck down Stone Cold Steve Austin at *Survivor Series*. Tired of

Rikishi nails The Rock with a superkick.

seeing Superstars such as Hulk Hogan and Austin thriving, the hate-filled Rikishi took out Stone Cold so that his fellow Samoan, The Rock, could become a megastar. The revelation not only shocked the fans, but also The Rock, who did not endorse the heinous act.

When Rikishi hit the ring at *No Mercy,* he immediately charged toward Angle. But the challenger was able to pull The Rock in front of him at the last moment, resulting in the champ absorbing much of the force. Rikishi followed up his first miscue with yet another when he connected with a superkick to The Rock's chin. This allowed the challenger to sweep in and hit his signature Angle Slam on The Rock for the win.

Just eleven months into his career, Angle had captured sports-entertainment's most coveted prize. Overcome by emotion, the new champ dropped to his knees and openly wept while clutching his new title. The scene was reminiscent of Shawn Michaels's *WrestleMania XII* victory. Only this time, fans failed to join in on the celebration. Instead, they simply rolled their eyes at the new champ, whose oversized ego was growing by the moment.

With the WWE Championship in his possession, Angle had the hardware necessary to back up his arrogant claims. And to the surprise of many, the relative newcomer also began picking up many monumental victories, including a win over the legendary Undertaker at November's *Survivor Series* and a Hell in a Cell triumph over five other men at *Armageddon* in December. With each passing win, Angle's in-ring prowess began to earn him the respect of the crowd. They still hated him, of course, but they couldn't help but appreciate his athleticism.

Down south, rival WCW answered with Pay-Per-View main events featuring Scott Steiner versus Booker T (November) and Steiner versus Sid Vicious (December). Sprinkled into the undercards of these events were such lackluster matches as Mike Sanders versus Kwee-Wee, Mancow versus Jimmy Hart, and General Rection versus Shane Douglas. Clearly, WCW was fading fast.

Rumors began to spread about the deteriorating company possibly being sold. In January 2001, those whispers became a reality when WCW.com announced that an Eric Bischoff–led consortium had acquired the company. The announcement, however, was premature. At the last moment, one of Bischoff's key components backed out, leaving WCW without a buyer.

Kurt Angle.

Back in WWE, Angle continued to roll. He defeated Triple H at the 2001 *Royal Rumble*, albeit with some help from Stone Cold, and was preparing to defend against The Rock at *No Way Out*. For Angle, a win against The Rock meant so much more than retaining the title. If he could beat the Brahma Bull, it would also give him a spot in the main event at *WrestleMania*, one of the few holes the champ still had on his résumé. The Rock, on the other hand, had already tasted the limelight of a *WrestleMania* main event, and he used that experience to defeat Angle following two Rock Bottoms.

The win gave the Brahma Bull his sixth WWE Championship and also reignited his epic rivalry with his upcoming *WrestleMania* opponent, Stone Cold. Over the next several weeks, The Rock and Austin successfully re-created the magic they had made two years prior heading into *Wrestle-Mania XV*. And like last time, fans could not get enough, as *Raw* ratings doubled what WCW's *Nitro* was pulling in. By this time, though, most of the star power had been drained from WCW, as evidenced by their two top titlists: An aged Rick Steiner was United States Champion, while his brother, Scott, was World Champ.

WCW was on its last legs. If somebody didn't step in and buy the company, many assumed they would simply have to close their doors. Luckily, it never got to that point, thanks to the shocking announcement that WWE had purchased its rival.

Fans learned of this on the historic March 26, 2001, *Raw-Nitro* simulcast, which was actually only a few hours after many in WCW's locker room heard the news. The Superstars were clearly stunned, but not by the sale itself. They had seen that coming years in advance.

"When the nWo kicked off, it was a great two years," says former WCW Superstar Kevin Nash. "Then Steve [Austin] and the Attitude Era got hot and things began to shift. Once things started going in WWE's direction, we knew we didn't stand a chance against Vince's production. We were always a TV company who did wrestling, where WWE was a wrestling company. I remember walking into TV the day after *WrestleMania XIV* and looking at Kevin Sullivan. He said, 'Brother, I put my hand in the water and it's getting cold. We're about to hit the iceberg.' That's when I knew the end was near."

Less than a week after the sale, a handful of WCW Superstars were invited to watch *WrestleMania X-Seven* from a skybox at the Reliant Astrodome. Their new boss, Shane McMahon, introduced them to the packed house, calling the rival wrestlers his "newfound friends." At that moment, it became painfully clear that the purchase of WCW was not fully embraced by a portion of WWE's fan base. Rather than cheering wildly at the introductions, many fans booed, while others refused to offer any response at all.

The reaction in the WWE locker room was also mixed. Some Superstars took great pride in helping their company win the Monday Night Wars, while others wished it never reached such a decisive conclusion, including one half of *WrestleMania X-Seven*'s main event, Stone Cold Steve Austin.

"It would've been great if they had stayed in business; I had a lot of fun there," admits Austin. "Me and Eric [Bischoff] buried the hatchet a long time ago. I don't have any animosity. My being fired actually turned out to be the greatest thing that ever happened to me. But I wish they were still hot right now. It would be some great competition. I really think there's enough room for everybody in this business."

Despite Austin's wishes, there was no room for a failing WCW in the 2001 sports-entertainment landscape. Poor business management, coupled with sinking ratings, made them a nonviable company. As a result, for the first time in WWE history, *WrestleMania* was broadcast without the threat of any competition. And its main event featured a WWE Championship Match between two of the greatest Superstars to ever lace a pair of boots— Steve Austin and The Rock.

At the time, both Stone Cold and The Rock were tremendous fan favorites. But because *WrestleMania X-Seven* was held in Texas, the crowd on this night heavily leaned toward Steve Austin, who hailed from Victoria, just two hours south of the Astrodome. In the end, it was this high level of admiration that made the night's final result so shocking and appalling.

With Stone Cold felled by a People's Elbow, The Rock went for the apparent match-ending cover. But before the three count could be completed, Mr. McMahon, of all people, interfered on Austin's behalf. He then handed a steel chair to his longtime enemy and watched as the Texas Rattlesnake viciously laid into the champion. From there, pinning The Rock was a mere formality. After the match, Austin and McMahon solidified their shocking union with a handshake and a few beers.

The victory gave Stone Cold his fifth WWE Championship. But on this night, nobody was talking about the title. Instead, everyone focused their attention on Steve Austin aligning himself with his archenemy, Mr. McMahon. At the time, the sight of Austin instantly transforming into McMahon's ally certainly provided for compelling television. In retrospect, however, many now disagree with the shocking decision, including Stone Cold who today admits that turning his back on the fans was not a wise career move.

On camera, Steve Austin's deal with the devil could not have come at a better time for Mr. McMahon. Just months after driving the old WCW into extinction, the new WCW led by Shane McMahon was threatening to return the favor. Behind the force of his "newfound friends," the younger McMahon devised a plan to extinguish the legacy his father had spent a lifetime building. But if he was going to be successful, he knew he was going to need more than just Booker T, Diamond Dallas Page, and the handful of other WCW names he had under contract. So he formed an alliance with ECW, which had just been acquired by his sister, Stephanie. The partnership added the likes of Rob Van Dam, Mike Awesome, and Lance Storm to Shane's quest to run his father out of business.

To fend off his children's partnership, Mr. McMahon formed an impressive combination of Superstars led by new ally and WWE Champion Steve Austin. Undertaker, Kane, Chris Jericho, and Kurt Angle joined Stone Cold for the highly anticipated showdown against the Alliance's Booker T, DDP, Rhyno, and the Dudleys at the *Invasion* Pay-Per-View. Heading into the event, many assumed Team WWE would prove their superiority and give Mr. McMahon the win he always gets when his back is against the wall. But those predictors failed to take into account one Superstar's bruised ego.

Feeling Mr. McMahon was favoring Kurt Angle over him, a disappointed Stone Cold actually turned against his own team at *Invasion* and nailed the Olympic gold medalist with a Stunner. The blow gave the Alliance what they needed to pick up the crucial victory. Even worse, Mr. McMahon's champion, the WWE Champion, had defected to WCW/ECW.

With the emotionally fragile Steve Austin now in the enemy camp, Mr. McMahon assigned Angle the heavy task of going into *Unforgiven* to

Chris Jericho.

bring the gold back home. Little did anybody know, Austin versus Angle would mean so much more than the WWE Championship.

Two weeks before *Unforgiven,* the United States was rocked by the tragic events of September 11, 2001. WWE fans and Superstars alike took a momentary step back from the rivalries to remember and respect those who had lost their lives on this senseless day. When the time was right, Americans slowly began to live their lives again, but it was an obvious struggle. They soon looked for a reason to smile again. And they needed a reason to cheer. WWE fans looking for an escape turned to their Olympic gold medalist and American hero, Kurt Angle.

With an entire nation of fans by his side, a red-white-and-blue-clad Angle defeated Steve Austin for the gold at *Unforgiven.* The win brought the championship back to WWE but, more important, provided America with some relief from the grieving that came after 9/11.

Kurt Angle's patriotic victory is a memory that will own permanent placement atop WWE's list of all-time great moments. His championship reign, on the other hand, was very temporary. Just two weeks after beating Stone Cold at *Unforgiven,* the Olympic gold medalist lost the title back to Austin on an episode of *Raw.* The win gave the Texas Rattlesnake his sixth WWE Championship reign, a record he shared with The Rock at the time.

Seeing his WWE Championship back around the waist of an Alliance Superstar infuriated Mr. McMahon, who finally looked to end the insanity by challenging his rival to a Winner-Take-All-Match at *Survivor Series.* Representing his team was Chris Jericho, Undertaker, Big Show, Kane, and The Rock. Team Alliance was comprised of new turncoat Kurt Angle, Booker T, Rob Van Dam, Shane McMahon, and WWE Champion Steve Austin. In the end, it was Angle turning on the Alliance and helping Team WWE get the win, thus ending WCW forever. (ECW returned a few years later, only to close shop again in early 2010.)

Finally, after decades of competition, there was only one true force in the sports-entertainment world: WWE. But there were two champions: WWE Champion Steve Austin and World Champion (formerly WCW Champion) The Rock. Believing there was no room for two champions in one company, Mr. McMahon announced a four-man tournament for *Vengeance.* In the first round, Austin would defend his title against Angle, while The

Rock would put his gold on the line against Jericho. The winners of those matches would advance to the finals, where WWE would crown the first-ever Undisputed World Champion.

Heading into *Vengeance,* many fans assumed they would see an Austin-Rock final. It just seemed natural, considering they were the two biggest names at the time, and both walked into the event as champions. Stone Cold kept up his end of the bargain by defeating Angle after a jaw-jacking Stunner. But The Rock surprisingly fell to Y2J, resulting in an Austin-Jericho final for the Undisputed WWE Championship.

"I don't have a lot of memories of the match other than I stunk," admits Austin. "I was living pretty fast at the time and I was just scrambled, both physically and mentally. That match was a complete phone-in job for me. And hell, I didn't even phone it in; I got hung up on. It was one of my worst matches ever. It didn't have anything to do with who I was in the ring with; I really like Jericho and consider him a friend. I was just frazzled and wanted the night to be over."

Thanks to some outside interference, it was over rather quickly. After a little more than ten minutes of action, Booker T nailed Stone Cold from behind with one of the championships, allowing Y2J to make the cover and become the first-ever Undisputed WWE Champion.

Even during WWE's earliest days, there was always a competing promotion whose champion could—right or wrong—claim ownership of the "real" world title. For Bruno Sammartino, it was the NWA's Lou Thesz. For Bob Backlund, it was the AWA's Nick Bockwinkel. For Hulk Hogan, it was the NWA/WCW's Ric Flair. But on this night, there was just WWE, and there was no disputing its claim to sports-entertainment's only world champion: Chris Jericho.

"It was the equivalent of winning an Oscar," says Y2J, reflecting on his groundbreaking place in history. "Nobody ever did it before, and it's something nobody could ever take away from me. That was such a huge honor for me, and I took it very seriously, especially with The Rock and Austin being involved."

25

UNDISPUTED

Chris Jericho's victory over Stone Cold Steve Austin at *Vengeance* gave the Canadian Superstar entry into WWE's most prestigious club—one he had nearly gained access to more than a year and a half earlier.

In April 2000, Y2J pinned Triple H's shoulders to the mat

to capture the WWE Championship on an episode of *Raw*. But only moments after the victory, The Game, claiming the three count was made too quickly, used his stroke to strong-arm referee Earl Hebner into reversing the decision, thus striking Jericho's championship win from the record books.

"Just the fact that I got to experience the taste of the title was amazing," recalls Jericho. "I had to give it back three segments later, but it didn't make a difference because it was the first time I got to wear it around my waist and experience being champion. Even though it wasn't officially recognized, the fans knew that something special had happened and it was their first glimpse of Chris Jericho climbing up the ladder. It was a great match too. The crowd was going insane. They exploded when I won the title, and that's all that matters."

This time, Jericho's title reign was for real, and to punctuate that fact, he quickly toppled two of the WWE's biggest names, The Rock and Austin, at the following two Pay-Per-Views. Y2J was on an unbelievable roll. But so was Triple H, despite the fact that doctors recently told him he might never wrestle again.

In May 2001, seven months before Jericho became Undisputed WWE Champion, The Game suffered a freak injury that severely jeopardized his in-ring career. "When I planted my left leg," said Triple H, "it felt like a lightning bolt hit me in the leg. And I felt my entire left quad muscle roll up my thigh."

Triple H had torn his quad completely off the bone. Making matters worse, everything surrounding his knee exploded. Renowned orthopedic surgeon Dr. James Andrews performed the complicated surgery, and he later told The Game that he had never seen anybody come back from an injury so severe.

With history working against him, a determined Triple H moved into a Birmingham, Alabama, hotel so he could work with his rehabilitation team seven days a week. WWE even sent a ring down so his physical therapists could watch him compete and identify which areas of his repertoire needed strengthening. After eight tireless months, the Cerebral Assassin finally returned to WWE on a January 2002 episode of *Raw* from Madison Square Garden.

"That was the biggest response I had ever heard in my life," says The Game. "It was deafening to me and it seemed to last forever."

It was here that Triple H announced that he was going to participate in the *Royal Rumble*, a match he ultimately won, which put him on a *WrestleMania* collision course with new Undisputed WWE Champion Chris Jericho.

For the second time in WWE history, *WrestleMania* traveled north of the border when Toronto, Ontario, Canada, played host to the eighteenth annual Pay-Per-View extravaganza. More than 68,000 fans packed into the SkyDome to witness firsthand one of the most star-studded lineups ever, which included on the undercard Ric Flair versus Undertaker, Stone Cold Steve Austin versus Scott Hall, and The Rock versus Hollywood Hulk Hogan.

"It's such an honor to be in the main event of *WrestleMania* as champion," says Jericho regarding his involvement in *WrestleMania X8*. "But on the same night was The Rock versus Hogan, which was like Ali versus Frazier. So in reality, Triple H and I were in the last match of the show, but the *real* main event was The Rock and Hogan. We were kind of like a main event with an asterisk."

The Rock versus Hogan certainly was a tough act to follow, but that didn't take any of the intensity away from *WrestleMania*'s first-ever Undisputed WWE Championship Match. Following some outside interference by Triple H's then-estranged wife, Stephanie, a Jericho victory appeared certain. But before the champ could put the finishing touches on the match, Triple H slyly managed to slip Y2J into a Pedigree for the win. The King of Kings had completed his quest. He was once again the WWE Champion.

26

HULK STILL RULES

Hulk Hogan's 2002 return to WWE didn't go exactly as planned. After leaving in 1993, the former fan favorite went to WCW, where he reinvented himself as one of sports-entertainment's greatest villains. So when he returned nearly ten years later, many, including the Hulkster, assumed he

would pick up where he left off as an antagonist. The fans had other plans. From the moment he appeared on-screen at *No Way Out* in February, the fans embraced him like it was 1985 all over. Unexpectedly, *Hulkamania* was running wild again.

According to the Hulkster, the original plan was for the aging Superstar to return for only a handful of dates alongside fellow New World Order members Kevin Nash and Scott Hall. But once Vince McMahon saw how positively the crowd responded to Hogan's homecoming, he asked the Hulkster to trade in his nWo black for the traditional red and yellow and placed him in several more high-profile encounters, including an Undisputed WWE Championship Match against Triple H at *Backlash* in April.

Eighteen years after defeating the Iron Sheik for his first WWE Championship, the forty-eight-year-old Hogan dropped his signature leg over the throat of The Game and pinned him to capture the sixth WWE title of his Hall of Fame career.

Lady Luck was certainly on Hogan's side at *Backlash*, especially considering Triple H was far and away the better competitor at that point in their respective careers. Not only did the Hulkster struggle to get his big boot up to The Game's chin level, but he also appeared to be in great pain while attempting the simplest of tasks, including walking.

As expected, it wasn't long before Hogan's luck ran out. Less than one month after capturing the title, the Hulkster was dethroned by the same Superstar who ended his third reign back in 1991: Undertaker. Ironically, in both instances, a steel chair was used to neutralize Hogan. This time, however, *Hulkamania* stayed down for good.

27

THE NEXT BIG THING

Undertaker successfully turned back Triple H at *King of the Ring* in 2002 before losing the gold to The Rock at *Vengeance*. As a result of the loss, the Deadman's reign failed to reach the two-month marker, but many fans never really recognized its brevity. Instead, their attention was focused on Brock

Lesnar, a monstrous newcomer so impressive he was tagged the Next Big Thing.

Prior to becoming the MMA sensation he is today, Lesnar perfected his in-ring skills as a member of WWE. He joined the roster in March 2002 and immediately turned heads with his unusual combination of size and superior technical wrestling skill. This unique union of attributes made him a threat to every Superstar in the WWE locker room, regardless of their fighting style.

Within months of his debut, Lesnar turned back the oversized Rikishi, speedy Jeff Hardy, and well-seasoned Booker T. He even defeated Rob Van Dam to capture the coveted *King of the Ring* crown in June. Thanks to the royal win, Lesnar was awarded an opportunity at The Rock's Undisputed WWE Championship at *SummerSlam*.

As the annual August spectacular neared, many assumed The Rock was simply keeping the title warm for Lesnar, who was decimating every opponent in his path, including Hulk Hogan. Hearing these whispers, the Undisputed WWE Champion started to train harder than ever before. To prove his dedication, he gave WWE cameras never-before-allowed access into his workouts, which included jumping hurdles, running ropes, shuttle drills, box jumps, Olympic lifts, and running the stairs at the Orange Bowl, his home stadium when he played college football for the University of Miami.

Unfortunately for The Rock, all his training was for naught. Despite entering *SummerSlam* in tremendous condition, he quickly learned that the Next Big Thing was not just a fancy nickname. After a fast-paced fourteen minutes of action, Lesnar dropped The Rock with an F-5 to become the youngest WWE Champion in history, at twenty-five years old.

At the time of Lesnar's victory, the Undisputed WWE Champion was expected to represent both *Raw* and *SmackDown* as their titlist. Unlike the rest of the WWE Superstars, who were required to stay on their designated brands, the champ was encouraged to jump from show to show and compete against any worthy roster member. Recognizing the drawing power of Lesnar, *Raw* General Manager Eric Bischoff planned a major evening for the new champion on the night following *SummerSlam*. But rival General Manager Stephanie McMahon, who also had big plans

Brock Lesnar.

for Lesnar, got to him first and signed him to an exclusive *SmackDown* contract.

Stephanie's shrewd signing of Lesnar left *Raw* without a champion . . . but only temporarily. One week after the new Undisputed WWE Champion left for *SmackDown*, Eric Bischoff announced that he was going to crown a new titlist to represent his brand, *Raw*. He then pulled out the classic WCW Championship, which many fans refer to as the "big gold belt," and awarded it to Triple H. With that one simple announcement, Bischoff had singlehandedly stripped the "undisputed" tag from Lesnar's championship, while introducing WWE to a second title known as the World Heavyweight Championship.

As an exclusive *SmackDown* commodity, Lesnar successfully defended the WWE Championship against newcomers Randy Orton and John Cena before entering into a vicious rivalry with Undertaker. The Deadman proved to be Lesnar's toughest task to date, but the champ miraculously managed to walk away with his reign intact after absorbing a bloody assault inside Hell in a Cell. But there was no rest for the weary. A showdown with the massive Big Show was looming.

Today's fans know that when Big Show hits the ring, it usually results in a win. But that wasn't always the case. After losing the WWE Championship to Triple H in January 2000, the World's Largest Athlete saw his career fall on some pretty hard times. Many within WWE began questioning his work ethic, especially after he became a comedy character specializing in impersonating other Superstars. The act drew laughs from crowds, but insiders knew that dressing up as Showkishi (Rikishi) and the Big Showbowski (the Big Valbowski) wasn't going to get him back into the main event picture. Finally, the former WCW and WWE Champion was sent down to Ohio Valley Wrestling, a developmental territory for young hopefuls.

"I was definitely in the outhouse, and it was frustrating. There were a lot of people frustrated in me, my performance, and my apparent dedication. I had insecurities back then. It was tough for me. It definitely wasn't from a lack of love for the business; I loved traveling and competing and being in the locker room. I just didn't know how to deal with my insecurities. And I didn't want to ask anybody for help because I didn't want to expose those insecurities. It wasn't until I went to [Ohio Valley Wrestling] that I started to ask for help. I aggravated the hell out of Triple H and Vince. I also had Fit Finlay and John Laurinaitis working with me every afternoon, trying to unleash the inner giant. Once we found all that and put it all together, we just moved forward. That's when I really started to understand."

With a new lease on life, Big Show returned to WWE in 2001 and spent the next several months proving himself all over again. After defeating the likes of Jeff Hardy, Rikishi, and former world champions Diamond Dallas Page and Booker T, he finally gained entry back into the main event scene. The night: *Survivor Series* 2002. The opponent: Brock Lesnar.

"I have a lot of respect for Brock," says Big Show. "He actually helped me get my career back in line again. The opinion of me wasn't really high at the time, nor did it deserve to be. I had a lot to prove, and Brock gave me that chance."

Once given the opportunity, Big Show refused to drop the ball. Utilizing an assist from Lesnar-turncoat Paul Heyman, the World's Largest Athlete was able to chokeslam his opponent onto a steel chair and pick up

the win. The victory successfully derailed one of the most impressive rookie campaigns of all time but, more important, reintroduced Big Show as a major player.

"That was my most memorable championship win," remembers Big Show. "Because of that, I've been able to go on to do many great things. It was the start of me getting the whole picture and becoming a *real* WWE Superstar."

Over the next eight years, Big Show went on to compete in some of sports-entertainment's biggest matches, including a battle with famed boxer Floyd "Money" Mayweather at *WrestleMania XXIV* and a Triple Threat World Heavyweight Championship Match against John Cena and Edge at *WrestleMania XXV*. But while the years that followed *Survivor Series* 2002 certainly helped paint a successful overall picture of Big Show's career, he did stumble a bit in the immediate moments following his WWE Championship victory. Just weeks after becoming a two-time titlist, the World's Largest Athlete was upended by Kurt Angle at *Armageddon*.

Kurt Angle's latest championship reign reemphasized the entertainment value of technical wrestling. Within weeks of capturing the gold, he competed in instant mat classics against both Rey Mysterio and Edge. Both matches amazed the fans; but little did they know, the best was yet to come.

When Brock Lesnar last eliminated Undertaker from the 2003 *Royal Rumble,* fans of pure mat wrestling began to salivate at the thought of the former NCAA heavyweight wrestling champion challenging Olympic gold medalist Angle for the WWE title at *WrestleMania XIX*. Never before had two such accomplished amateurs squared off in the main event of sports-entertainment's crown jewel.

Unbeknownst to the fans, Lesnar versus Angle at *WrestleMania* almost never happened. In the weeks leading up to the event, Angle suffered a serious neck injury, making it nearly impossible for him to compete. As a result, he was forced to make the most difficult decision of his career: risk permanent injury at *WrestleMania* or vacate the WWE Championship. Ultimately, Angle chose to keep the gold and fight through the pain, knowing that he would be risking further injury and that surgery would be required immediately afterward.

As expected, the match heavily featured moves from each Superstar's amateur wrestling background. Recognizing they were witnessing great-ness, the sold-out Safeco Field in Seattle, Washington, cheered wildly with each armbar, headlock, and fireman's carry—moves that don't normally elicit a response, but when strung together like this, it was impossible for the crowd not to show their appreciation.

Lesnar nailed Angle with an F-5 late in the match. But rather than go for the cover, he uncharacteristically climbed to the top rope. From there, he leapt high in the air, flipping himself over in the process in an attempt to hit a shooting star press. Unfortunately for Lesnar, he failed to com-plete the flip, resulting in him landing directly on his head. The audience gasped, hoping he was all right, while color commentator Tazz questioned, "How is Lesnar not dead right now?" More than seven years later, Lesnar's botched shooting star press remains a classic *WrestleMania* moment that is still talked about regularly. Miraculously, Lesnar was able to pull himself together and nail Angle with another F-5 to finally pick up the win in his first-ever *WrestleMania*.

In the past, injuries such as Kurt Angle's kept Superstars out of action for one full year. But thanks to an uncommon surgical procedure conducted

by world-renowned neurosurgeon Dr. Hae-Dong Jho, Angle was able to return to the ring after just four short months. And unlike his predecessors, he bounced back as good as new, reclaiming the WWE Championship his first time out at *Vengeance*. Unfortunately for Angle, however, his time back on top was fleeting. A mere two months into his reign, Lesnar struck again. This time he topped Angle in a thrilling sixty-minute WWE Iron Man Match on *SmackDown*.

On the surface, Lesnar's third reign seemed extremely satisfying for the young Superstar. But behind the scenes, living out of a suitcase and waking up in a different city every morning was starting to take a toll on the WWE Champion, and he quietly began to question if a future in the ring was what he really wanted.

News of Lesnar's unhappiness began to spread throughout the locker room, which disappointed many Superstars. They couldn't understand how he could have thoughts of leaving after everything WWE had done for him. The company had spent millions of dollars in television time, marketing efforts, and merchandising to help make him a star, but for a reason incomprehensible to them, he didn't seem to want the spotlight WWE was providing.

A small percentage of Lesnar's colleagues actually understood, though, including longtime rival Big Show: "Some people can't take the schedule. They crack. I've seen it on the plane; I've seen them get to a town, go to the locker room, and break down crying because they can't handle the schedule. In Brock's case, it's sad because there was a lot of effort put into making him a star, and for whatever reason, he decided it wasn't for him. He had to do what he had to do. That was his decision. He had all the tools to be one of the greatest champions ever, but to be really great in this business, you have to love it more than anything else. Some people just aren't prepared to make that sacrifice."

Lesnar forged on for several more months. Over that time, he successfully defended his WWE Championship against Undertaker and Hardcore Holly, among others. Amazingly, despite his discontent, Lesnar managed to look unstoppable along the way. Then came Eddie Guerrero.

28

EDDIE

Every WWE Championship victory is special in its own distinct

way. For Eddie Guerrero, his was the culmination of an inspi-

rational battle back from desolation and hopelessness.

As the son of lucha libre legend Gory Guerrero, and

younger brother to wrestlers Hector, Mando, and Chavo,

Eddie's career path was paved for him well before he even learned to walk. He spent his earliest days observing his father promote shows at the El Paso Coliseum in Texas. When he was old enough, he helped set up the ring, pass out flyers, sell concessions ... anything that would help his father, as well as keep him out of the competitors' hair. He loved to rub elbows with the big names that passed through town, such as Ernie Ladd and El Santo.

Back home, Guerrero honed his craft in the ring his family had set up in their backyard. His older brothers were amazed at how quickly he picked it up. He was a natural. In his 2005 autobiography, *Cheating Death, Stealing Life*, Guerrero admitted, "I've always had an aptitude for wrestling. I can't explain it—it's like a gift."

Guerrero's gift propelled him to the professional circuit in June 1987, at the young age of nineteen. He teamed with the masked Matematico to defeat El Vikingo and Flama Roja in his debut match at the Auditorio Municipal in Juarez, Mexico. For the next several years, he bounced around several different Mexican promotions, as well as Japan, before getting his first big United States opportunity in 1995.

Extreme Championship Wrestling's Paul Heyman had seen Guerrero's work and asked if he would be interested in competing at some shows in Philadelphia. Guerrero had always dreamed of working in the States, but he thought his smaller stature and ethnicity would prevent it from ever happening. Heyman didn't care about his size or where he was from, though; instead, he saw a competitor with a pure wrestling ability second to none. It was exactly what ECW needed: amazing in-ring skills to help offset the hardcore battles for which the promotion was becoming known.

The hard-to-impress ECW fans became instantly enamored with Guerrero's impeccable performances. It wasn't long before the Eddie Guerrero name started to gain fame outside of ECW's Philadelphia footprint. Even those in WCW's executive offices in Atlanta were forced to take notice. After only a few months with ECW, WCW booker Kevin Sullivan called Guerrero to offer him a job. At the time, WCW was preparing for the launch of *Monday Nitro* and was looking for guys who knew how to wrestle, as opposed to the older competitors they had at the top of the card, such as Hulk Hogan and Randy Savage.

Eddie Guerrero was on top of the world. Not only did working for

WCW give him national exposure, but it also meant more money than he had ever earned before. Not surprisingly, he gained great success in the WCW ring, complete with two Cruiserweight Championship reigns and one run with the United States title. But the politics that went along with being WCW property caused painful amounts of stress. Guerrero began partying to help numb the pain. With each passing day of his WCW tenure, Guerrero spiraled more and more out of control.

All the partying started to take a toll on Guerrero's marriage as well. His wife, Vickie, begged for him to get his life back in order, but he refused to listen, and the once-happy couple became locked in a constant argument. After a New Year's Eve fight in 1999, an upset and inebriated Guerrero jumped in his TransAm and made his way down Highway 54. Recklessly, he got the car up to 130 miles per hour before passing out behind the wheel. With Guerrero unconscious in the driver's seat, the car jumped off an embankment and began soaring through the air. By the time it landed, the car was an unrecognizable mess, with many parts still stuck up in the trees.

Guerrero was taken to the hospital via helicopter. When Vickie arrived, the doctors told her that her husband probably wouldn't make it through the next two nights. And if he miraculously did, he certainly would never wrestle again. They were wrong on both points.

Unfortunately, the accident failed to serve as a wakeup call. Guerrero began abusing painkillers to help ease the aches that go along with crashing a car at 130 miles per hour. He eventually overdosed and wound up nearly lifeless in a hospital bed on several occasions. The only shining light was that WCW had finally granted him his release.

Guerrero's personal life was in a shambles. He was wise enough, though, to hide his problems from the public and, more important WWE, who agreed to hire the free agent in 2000. As a WWE Superstar, Guerrero had finally gained the global recognition a top-notch competitor deserves. Behind the scenes, however, he was continuing to unravel. Vickie finally grew tired of babysitting her husband and asked for a divorce. Shortly afterward, WWE learned of Guerrero's demons and ordered him to enter a four-month rehabilitation program. He hated the idea of being away from his children for so long, but he ultimately agreed.

Rehab did little to defeat Guerrero's addictions, and it wasn't long before he was back on the bottle. In late 2001, he woke up on a jail cell floor after being arrested for drinking and driving. This latest incident cost him his last shred of normalcy. He had already lost his family and finances, and when Vince McMahon learned of the arrest, he lost his job as well. Guerrero had hit rock bottom.

Guerrero began wrestling on the independent circuit after being released from WWE, which meant the size of the crowd he competed in front of shrunk from 20,000 to 200. His paycheck experienced a similar decrease. At this point, it would have been easy for Guerrero to sink deeper into despair. Miraculously, however, he found it within himself to fight for what he had lost. It took hitting rock bottom for him to realize a drastic change needed to be made. Not only did he commit himself to sobriety, but he also began training harder than ever before. It wasn't long before he was in the best shape of his life.

After six months of humility and sobriety, Guerrero got the call to return to WWE. He capped off his return by defeating Rob Van Dam for the Intercontinental Championship only three weeks into his second chance. The victory was a product of living life the right way and giving one hundred percent in the ring, something he admitted to not doing during his first stint with WWE.

On February 15, 2004, a revitalized Guerrero put the ultimate exclamation point on his return when he defeated Brock Lesnar at *No Way Out* to capture the WWE Championship. Prior to that match, his legacy could very easily have been one of countless car accidents, overdoses, arguments, and jail, hospital, and rehab stays. But when he held the WWE Championship high for the very first time, all that negativity washed away. He had forever rewritten his legacy. He was Eddie Guerrero, the WWE Champion.

GUERRERO REMEMBERS THE MATCH IN HIS AUTOBIOGRAPHY:

Though I'd worked my entire life for this moment, nothing could've prepared me for the reality. I was the WWE Champion! I'd reached the top of the wrestling mountain! There is no greater honor in this business.

I had beaten Brock Lesnar, a great champion almost twice my size, in an arena overflowing its capacity with fans, most of whom

were Chicanos there to see me, Latino Heat, try to win the biggest match of my career.

It was truly an amazing night, made even more incredible by the fact that just two and a half years earlier I wasn't even working for WWE. I'd been let go after my lifetime of drug and alcohol addiction had finally sent me hurtling to the lowest point of my entire life.

If someone had told me then that I was going to be the standard bearer for World Wrestling Entertainment, the biggest and best wrestling company on the planet, I would never have believed it.

Nobody—not even myself—had ever seen me as a main eventer, as a guy who could be trusted to represent the best a wrestling promotion had to offer. It was Vince, God bless him, who really believed in me. And his faith in me gave me the confidence to go out and give Brock Lesnar the match of my life.

Guerrero had little time to relish his WWE Championship victory. Earlier that same night, Kurt Angle had defeated Big Show and John Cena to become the number-one contender for the title. As a result, Guerrero would defend his newly won title at *WrestleMania XX* against former four-time WWE Champion and Olympic gold medalist Angle.

In the nineteen years prior, only the best of the best battled for the WWE Championship at *WrestleMania*—Andre the Giant, Hulk Hogan, Ric Flair, Bret Hart—and on this night, the two best in the business were Guerrero and Angle. With plans of eventually cinching in his signature Angle Lock, Angle focused much of his offense on the lower portion of Guerrero's leg. But when the time finally came for Angle to lock in the hold, he unexpectedly pulled the champ's boot from his foot, causing him to stumble backward. This allowed Guerrero to swoop in and roll up the shocked Angle for the win.

"I was very happy with the match," claimed Guerrero in his autobiography, "though I don't think it was as great as people have told me it was. Still, it was pretty thrilling, defending the WWE title at *WrestleMania*, in Madison Square Garden."

JBL had been with WWE for eight years. He enjoyed moderate success during his run, mostly as a cowboy or beer-swilling brawler, but he was never able to achieve main event status. Then in March 2004, shortly after Eddie Guerrero defeated Kurt Angle at *WrestleMania*, JBL traded in his cutoff T-shirts for an expensive suit and fancy limousine. The change in appearance was exactly what his career needed.

"I was basically a Vince McMahon who wrestled," says JBL. "I think Vince saw it as a way for a rich guy, who had an identical persona to him, to be able to get in the ring and do the things that he couldn't do because of both time and being on the road. His commitments to WWE and the fact that he was older prevented him from doing it. We used to laugh about it all the time. I can't speak for Vince, but I think a lot of it was Vince living vicariously through JBL."

With the new persona also came an annoying level of arrogance for JBL. Claiming his mountains of money and American citizenship made him better than most, he began to take shots at anybody with a pulse, most notably "border-crossing" Mexicans.

JBL's verbal barbs eventually led to a thrilling series of WWE Championship matches. Eddie Guerrero was able to get past the first with his reign intact, but the Texas Bullrope Match at the *Great American Bash* proved to be considerably more difficult. After more than twenty minutes of using the rope and its rusty cowbell as a weapon, a mangled JBL managed to eke out the win to capture the WWE Championship.

The loss marked the end of the greatest four months of Eddie Guerrero's career. Tragically, the world lost Guerrero the following year when he passed away at the age of thirty-eight from congenital heart disease. Though gone, he would never be forgotten, especially by his peers, who would always remember him as a true champion.

STEPHANIE McMAHON ON THE *RAW* TRIBUTE SHOW: I talked to Eddie on Friday and we had a quick conversation and in that conversation Eddie had told me that he was going to be WWE Champion again or he was going to be the World Champion again and he wanted me to know that. He wanted Vince to know that. He was going to be champion again.

And when I think of Eddie, the most important thing that I think about is his family because he loved his family more than any-

thing else in the world, from his brothers to his mother, but especially his wife, Vickie. He loved you so much, Vickie. And Shaul and Sheri-lyn, he lit up when he talked about you. He just lit up. You were his whole life, his whole world. And I just hope that you guys know that. And I am so sorry.

Eddie Guerrero was a son. He was a husband. He was a father and he was a friend. And now Eddie will always, always be a cham-pion. I'll miss you, Eddie. Everybody will miss you. We love you.

29

A WRESTLING GOD

John Bradshaw Layfield's WWE Championship victory over Eddie Guerrero at the *Great American Bash* shocked the sports-entertainment world. At the time he was approaching forty, with his best years becoming a fading memory. And even when he was at his best, he was seen by many as nothing more than a midcard Superstar.

JBL with Cabinet members Orlando Jordan and Amy Weber.

"There were several times during the course of my career that I thought it would never happen for me," says JBL, "especially around 1997 when the guy who was head of creative [Vince Russo] just didn't like me. He didn't really see much value in me. He stuck me and Ron Simmons together because, as he put it, 'What else do they have to do?' If things stayed the same for me, there's no way I would've ever had the WWE Championship run."

Things briefly began to look up for JBL following Russo's departure

from WWE. But a string of bad luck set him back once again. In 2002, JBL was in line for a series of high-profile matches with Stone Cold Steve Austin. The rivalry would've assuredly elevated the struggling Superstar to heights he had never reached before. But right before they were able to square off, Austin quit, leaving JBL out of the biggest opportunity of his career. With Stone Cold out, the big Texan was forced back into the now-defunct hardcore division, where he regularly battled perennial midcarders Johnny Stamboli, Justin Credible, and Shawn Stasiak.

JBL also fought the injury bug, but he battled back each time. Eventually, his number was called again.

"When I tore my biceps, I wondered if I would ever get back in the ring," says JBL. "My good years were behind me, and I didn't know if it would be worth it coming back. But good fortune smiled on me because of the bad fortune of others—Big Show was hurt, Undertaker was hurt, Kurt Angle was hurt, Brock [Lesnar] had just left the company. They needed a guy immediately to step up against Eddie Guerrero, and fortunately, I was in the right place at the right time."

The right place was Norfolk, Virginia. The right time was June 27, 2004. Just moments before JBL walked out to face Guerrero for the WWE Championship, Pat Patterson turned to him and said, "I hope you do well out there . . . for your sake." Even then, minutes before he would have the title wrapped firmly around his waist, JBL was still being met with criticism. But he didn't let it bother him. Instead, he drew upon past experiences to help get through the gigantic match.

"I remembered going back to the first time I wrestled Kevin Von Erich for the NWA Championship fifteen years before," recalls JBL. "I remembered being overwhelmed by the match. It was a horrible match, not because of Kevin, but because of me. I was in awe of both Kevin and the magnitude of the match. Heading into the match with Eddie, I remember thinking no matter what was going to happen, I was going to go out there and be myself. Sink or swim, it was going to work."

JBL was right: He defeated Guerrero for the WWE Championship, a feat many thought he could never accomplish.

"It was unbelievable, especially after I struggled for so long. I broke in back in the old circuit days, wrestling in the carnivals in Europe. Becoming WWE Champion was something I didn't think would ever happen. It was something that I always wanted, but I thought it had passed me by."

After using some help from Kurt Angle to defeat Guerrero in a Steel Cage rematch on *SmackDown*, JBL was met with the gravest threat to his new reign—Undertaker. Over the next several months, JBL managed to narrowly escape the Phenom's deadly clutches on several occasions, thanks to the help of his Cabinet, Orlando Jordan and the Basham Brothers. Eventually, the dastardly way in which the champ eked by Undertaker started to wear on fans.

"I enjoyed being a bad guy," brags JBL, more than five years later. "A lot of people had a hard time being a bad guy, but my success was in the character. I preferred leaving the arena and having people throw things at my car and tell me that I didn't deserve to be WWE Champion. I really wanted to get under people's skin, and I think I did. I understood that character very well; I saw it a million times growing up—the rich old guy who threw money at everybody's nose, but you couldn't do anything about it because he owned the town.

"I think walking to the ring in a jacket with a towel around my neck really got under people's skin too. I got the idea for that in the gym—I was sitting there and saw this guy walking around in a jacket and towel. I remember thinking how mad it made me—I wanted to slap him. And then I thought, 'Hey, that's what JBL would do.' So I did it.

"What a lot of people don't understand is that JBL has no redeeming qualities . . . zero. Plus, he was *not* a good wrestler. I broke in while in Japan. I knew how to wrestle. But later in my career, there were times when I just didn't have the physical ability."

JBL took being hated by the fans to a whole new level. To him, it was an art form. He carefully calculated his every move. It was important that he never did anything to warrant adulation from the fans. He even admits to intentionally competing at a lower level than his opponents so that when he finally did win, the fans would become even more irate. This gave them a false sense of security—a belief that their favorite was going to topple the self-proclaimed "Wrestling God." "That was the key to my success," reflects JBL.

By the 2005 *Royal Rumble*, JBL had earned the distinction of being the longest reigning WWE Champion since Shawn Michaels's first reign back in 1996. It was an amazing accomplishment for a man many thought was too old to be champion. Closing in on forty, the former midcarder was quickly becoming owner of one of the most successful WWE Championship reigns in recent history.

The success of the rejuvenated JBL continued at the *Royal Rumble*, where the champ once again used some help from his Cabinet to dispose of Kurt Angle and Big Show in a Triple Threat Match. While the victory was certainly huge for JBL, it was somewhat overshadowed by WWE's next generation of champions—Batista and John Cena—who emerged as the final two combatants of the *Royal Rumble* match.

With a trip to *WrestleMania 21* on the line, Batista delivered a devastating spinebuster to John Cena before finally throwing him over the top for the win. With the victory, the Animal was awarded the right to choose which title he wanted to challenge for at *WrestleMania*: JBL's WWE Championship or Triple H's World Heavyweight Championship. Many assumed he would select the WWE title, considering his then-allegiance to The Game. But Batista shocked everyone when he went against the grain and elected to face his faction mate Triple H.

When Batista decided to take on The Game, not only did he effectively sever all ties with Evolution, but he also left an opening for another Superstar to slip in and challenge JBL for the WWE Championship at *WrestleMania*. That void was eventually filled by Cena, who outlasted Orlando Jordan, Booker T, and Kurt Angle in a number-one contenders' tournament to earn his first of what would eventually become many *WrestleMania* main events.

30

THE CHAMP IS HERE

Over the course of *WrestleMania*'s twenty-year history, it had

become customary for the WWE Champion to close the show.

Many saw it as a sign of respect reserved specifically for the

holder of WWE's flagship title and his opponent. Understand-

ably, when JBL learned his title defense wasn't going to close

WrestleMania 21, he was more than a little miffed. But not because he wouldn't be afforded the spotlight.

"No offense to the guys in the main event, but I think it was a horrible mistake not to let John Cena close the show that night," says JBL. "It was clear Cena was going to be the guy to carry the company, and he deserved to close. I said it at the time, but they disagreed with me. In hindsight, I think they would probably agree with me now."

John Cena, on the other hand, was just happy to be a part of the WWE Championship Match. It didn't matter if it was first, last, or somewhere in between.

The match ended up happening just prior to the night's final contest— Triple H versus Batista. After an extravagant entrance that saw fake $100 bills fall from the ceiling, JBL instantly jumped on the offensive. He maintained that momentum through the first nine minutes of the match. But despite his constant offensive onslaught, he couldn't keep John Cena's shoulders down for the three count. Finally, JBL went for the kill with his signature Clothesline from Hell, but Cena countered it into an Attitude Adjustment for the win, thus ending JBL's epic ten months atop the WWE roster.

"I regret that I didn't have more gas in my tank," says JBL. "A lot of guys are able to compete in the ring until they are forty-five or even older. But my time came a lot earlier because of all the injuries. I think I could've done a lot of stuff over the next few years based solely on that championship run. But my body gave out on me, which I regret. But then again, I guess if it happened earlier in my career, I wouldn't have had the mental acumen as far as wrestling is concerned to handle it. I learned a lot during that championship reign, and I thought I already knew a lot."

Unlike such timeless classics as Shawn Michaels versus Bret Hart (*WrestleMania XII*) or Eddie Guerrero versus Kurt Angle (*WrestleMania XX*), JBL versus John Cena was fought at a very slow and methodical pace, resulting in many historians choosing not to list it as an all-time great *WrestleMania* match. The slight might bother some Superstars. Not Cena, though. In fact, he doesn't even remember the match.

"My week was so busy. Literally, I was everywhere at once all week

long. I just remember that after it was done, I had the WWE Championship. It went by so fast I didn't really have the chance to put it all in perspective."

Things got even busier for John Cena following *WrestleMania 21*. Not only did he need to fulfill his commitments as WWE Champion, both in and out of the ring, but his debut hip-hop album also dropped shortly after, resulting in twice the public appearances. But Cena never batted an eye. Instead, he made a commitment to himself to make both his reign and his album as successful as possible. And from a distance, his peers looked on in pure amazement.

"John Cena is a prime example of what it means to be champion," says Big Show. "I don't think he even goes home. Whether you like him or not, you're not going to outwork him. The kid doesn't know surrender, and that's not just a slogan for his T-shirt. John Cena can run eight weeks in a row, not go home, and still outwork everyone around him, all with a smile on his face. That's a real credit to the kind of guy he is and the work ethic he has."

Cena's tireless efforts helped *You Can't See Me* debut at number fifteen on the *Billboard* charts. Amazingly, the champ also found time to ditch the traditional WWE Championship belt and design a completely new look. Like most of its predecessors, the new version featured an eagle draped across the top. But in the center there was a giant diamond-encrusted WWE logo that spun. Referred to as the "spinner belt," the new-look title was frowned upon by traditionalists, who believed the WWE Championship should be simply stated and void of all bling.

"Those traditionalists should watch some old matches from the 1950s and tell me they are exciting," Cena retorts. "This business is evolutionary. As a company, as a brand, and as a champion, I wanted to move forward and start a new tradition."

Eventually, John Cena's extracurricular activities began to rub fans the wrong way. In the past, they could count on their champion defending against the roster's most worthy competitors. But ever since Cena won the title, he only managed to earn a few victories over less accomplished Superstars such as Orlando Jordan and René Duprée. He had yet to truly put an in-ring stamp on his reign.

Judgment Day was Cena's opportunity to prove he had the in-ring wherewithal to be WWE Champion. Competing against JBL in an "I Quit"

Match, he absorbed a DDT on the arena floor, being abused with a leather belt, having his head rammed with a microphone, and being bloodied by a steel chair. It was a punishment Cena had never felt before, but he still refused to say "I quit."

Instead, the bloodied champ sent JBL crashing through a nearby table before threatening to ram him with a steel exhaust pipe. At that moment, JBL chose to live to fight another day. He grabbed the microphone from the referee and screamed the two most humiliating words any Superstar could say, "I quit!"

The win gave Cena his first Pay-Per-View victory as WWE Champion. But more important, it also solidified him as a great champion in the eyes of many, but not all.

"I think I'm still working on convincing everybody of my worth," says Cena. "I'm glad people still talk about that match and I'm glad they enjoyed it. But this is a very finicky profession, very what-have-you-done-for-me-lately. So you can never rest on what you've done. You're expected to prove your worth every single day."

A few weeks after *Judgment Day*, Cena was forced to prove himself against an entirely new roster when he was drafted from *SmackDown* to *Raw*. Predraft stipulations allowed him to take the WWE Championship with him, which clearly caused *Raw*'s existing Superstars to salivate at the thought of challenging for the title. But the change in scenery did little to slow down the white-hot Cena. The wins kept piling up for him, and as the calendar began to close on 2005, Kurt Angle, Shawn Michaels, and Randy Orton all became victims of the champ. But as the new year emerged, so did a new challenge.

In his final act as *Raw* General Manager, Eric Bischoff announced that Cena would defend the WWE Championship against HBK, Angle, Chris Masters, Carlito, and Kane in an Elimination Chamber Match at *New Year's Revolution*. With six Superstars all vying for the same prize, the percentages were certainly working against the champ. But just as he did so many times in the past, Cena overcame the adversity and battled through a grueling thirty minutes of abuse to retain his title.

The referee draped the gold over the exhausted champ's beaten body, signifying the end of the event.

Mr. McMahon, however, had other ideas.

"Don't go anywhere," he announced to the audience. "Nobody goes anywhere. This night is not over. Raise the cage!"

The confused ring crew looked at McMahon dumbfounded.

"Raise the cage, I said!"

The Elimination Chamber finally began to ascend toward the ceiling, as a weakened Cena struggled to get to his feet.

"The reason this night is not over will become apparent in a moment. First of all, I would like to congratulate John Cena on retaining the WWE Championship. [But] there's one more match to happen here tonight. And this individual is cashing in his Money in the Bank privilege that he earned at *WrestleMania*. The WWE Championship Match will take place right here, right now. *John Cena defends against Edge*."

With Cena still on the mat, Edge handed his briefcase to McMahon and made his way to the ring. The exhausted champ finally found the strength to stand as the bell rang, signifying the start of yet another title defense. A mere two minutes later, it was all over. Edge had flattened Cena with two spears to claim the WWE title.

For Edge, a self-admitted Hulkamaniac, the victory was the realization of a lifelong dream. Growing up in Toronto, he fantasized about one day following in his hero's footsteps. And on this night, after more than a decade of competing professionally, his dream finally came true. As he reached for his newly won title, a wave of emotions overcame the champ.

"The magnitude of the situation took over and I began to well up. When I heard the announcement, it was all so surreal. I had to stop and ask myself, 'Is this for real? Is this really happening to me?' "

When the new champ reached the locker room, he called his mother to share the good news.

"She was there through all the steps along the way. She was there for my first-ever match and she was there for my first WWE match. She was there for all those special moments. My only regret was that she wasn't there that day. That's why I made sure she was my first call."

In retrospect, it was probably best that she wasn't there; she definitely would not have approved of what her son did next. After hanging up with his mother, Edge and girlfriend Lita went on WWE.com to declare they were going to celebrate the win by having "hot, nasty sex" the next night on *Raw*.

The infamous live sex celebration on *Raw*.

"It was my job to push buttons. If people were offended, it meant I was doing my job. The ratings also proved that."

The lewd act registered an amazing 5.2 rating, which was the highest rating for a *Raw* ending in more than two years. Edge's popularity also resulted in twenty-five million WWE.com page views in just twenty-four hours. The combination of his television and online success gave the Rated-R Superstar every right to call himself the most-watched WWE Champion of all time. The only problem was that he wasn't going to be champion for long. On January 29, 2006, John Cena forced Edge to tap out to an STF at the *Royal Rumble*, thus ending his meteoric rise to the top.

"Without a doubt, I was very frustrated at that point," says Edge. "But I took that frustration and channeled it into motivation. I wanted to show them that they should've had me in the main event at *WrestleMania*. So I went out there [against Mick Foley at *WrestleMania 22*] and I went through a flaming table and I landed on thumbtacks and I made sure they knew that I was there and I belonged in the main event."

While Edge was competing in a Hardcore Match against Mick Foley at *WrestleMania*, John Cena was busy defending his WWE Championship against Triple H in the main event—the match Edge believed he deserved. Cena defeated The Game that night to retain the title, but while he certainly had reason to celebrate, the results of an earlier match that night would later come back to haunt his reign. In the night's second contest, Rob Van Dam outlasted five other Superstars to capture the Money in the Bank briefcase, meaning he could challenge Cena for the WWE Championship any time, any place.

Like Edge—the original Mr. Money in the Bank—RVD opted not to cash in his WWE title opportunity right away. Instead, he wisely sat back and waited, carefully assessing when the champ would be at his most vulnerable. Then, when WWE announced they were going to hold an ECW Pay-Per-View at New York's Hammerstein Ballroom—an old ECW stomping ground—RVD saw his opening. Realizing he would have the support of the entire arena, the ECW Original challenged Cena to a WWE Championship Match.

A barrage of boos rained down on the champ as he entered the Ballroom for *One Night Stand*. For John Cena, a mixed reaction was commonplace in WWE arenas. But this was far from mixed. Nearly all of the ECW crowd was firmly stationed in RVD's corner.

"The negative vibe they came out with for me was fantastic," remembers Cena. "It made for one of the better atmospheres ever seen. I loved every second of it. It was ECW purists rooting for one of their own."

Prior to the start of the match, John Cena tossed his hat and shirt into the crowd, thinking they would make great souvenirs for a few lucky fans. The ECW faithful, however, weren't on the same page as the champ. They wanted no part of the enemy's gear, so they threw both items back into the ring. Assuming this may have been an isolated act carried out by two rogue fans, Cena picked up the items and threw them back into the crowd. The fans threw them back into the ring again. This went on for several minutes, delaying the start of the match. They even tossed rolls of toilet paper at the champ—a not-so-subtle sign of what they thought of him.

Rob Van Dam victorious.

The unrelenting verbal assault continued throughout the start of the match and beyond. Amazingly, Cena managed to ignore the onslaught while controlling much of the offense during the contest. It wasn't until Edge, whose identity was disguised by a motorcycle helmet and long black trench coat, interfered that RVD saw his first true winning opportunity. While Van Dam was recovering from being dumped out of the ring, Edge ran in and speared Cena through a table. When the challenger finally regained his composure, he noticed the champ laid out in the middle of the ring and began to capitalize. He jumped to the top rope and hit his patented Five-Star Frog Splash. Paul Heyman then ran in and made the match-ending three count. In front of a rabid ECW crowd, Rob Van Dam, whom many considered the greatest wrestler never to hold a world championship, finally climbed to the top of the sports-entertainment industry. After the match, the new champ celebrated throughout the Ballroom, including the balcony, where his wife had watched the historic night unfold.

RVD's victory coincided with the fulltime re-launch of the ECW brand, which provided for some initial confusion. Paul Heyman proclaimed that Van Dam would simply take the WWE Championship and rechristen it the ECW Championship. But RVD decided to keep both titles separate, stating that the ECW title was a huge honor, but the WWE title, as he jokingly put it, "spins."

RVD's decision to defend both titles made him the first-and-only Superstar to hold both the ECW and WWE Championships simultaneously. ECW loyalists lauded RVD's unique place in history, but they soon received an unfortunate dose of reality that dashed their dreams of a WWE takeover. On July 2, 2006, Van Dam and fellow ECW Superstar Sabu were pulled over for speeding and ultimately arrested for possession of drugs in Ohio. As a result, both Superstars were handed thirty-day suspensions in accordance with the WWE wellness program.

The few days prior to RVD's suspension taking effect may have been the worst of his professional career. After spending more than a decade and a half clawing for the WWE and ECW Championships, he saw both his titles disappear in a matter of hours. On July 3, 2006—one day after his arrest—Van Dam lost the WWE Championship to Edge in a *Raw* Triple Threat Match that also included Cena. Twenty-four hours later, he lost the ECW Championship to Big Show.

Shortly after bringing the gold back home from its brief stay in the Land of the Extreme, Edge surprisingly asked girlfriend Lita to toss the prestigious title into the grimy Long Island Sound. This greatly infuriated the title's designer, John Cena, who viciously attacked the Rated-R Superstar. The assault eventually spilled over into the crowd before making its way outside the arena and back toward the Sound. WWE officials did their best to separate the two. But there was no stopping Cena. He finally tossed Edge into the same murky waters that the WWE Championship had gone into earlier that night.

An irate Edge demanded Cena be fired for his blatant disrespect toward the champion. But before a decision could be rendered, Cena made an offer to the Rated-R Superstar he could not refuse. As expected, he asked for a rematch with Edge, but he raised the stakes by agreeing to leave *Raw* forever if he could not win back the gold. Seeing this as his opportunity to rid himself of John Cena once and for all, Edge agreed to the rematch, but he also added a stipulation of his own: The contest would take place under TLC rules at *Unforgiven* in the champ's hometown of Toronto.

In Canada, Edge is recognized as a national hero. Proud to see one of their own make it big, Canadians manage to look past all of Edge's despicable traits and show him unconditional support each and every time he competes in their arenas. On this night, the locale was the Air Canada Centre, and they cheered him wildly upon his announcement.

"My real emotions came out that night," remembers Edge. "If you go back and watch the match, you can see me trying to hold that emotion back when I was announced. I had all of these different thoughts swirling around in my head. It was just really amazing for me, a lifelong fan, to be able to go into the ACC and defend the title in the main event of my hometown in a TLC Match."

Ironically, Cena, who was met with a reception similar to the one he received at ECW *One Night Stand*, also found pleasure in being part of Edge's homecoming.

"That was a really enjoyable moment for me," says Cena. "To see the kid who grew up idolizing WWE be in a championship match in his hometown was a lot of fun."

The fun stopped once the bell rang, especially for Edge, who admits to being legitimately knocked out during the contest.

"John had me in the [Attitude Adjustment] when I was trapped in the ladder," says Edge. "And that's the last thing I remember. I just blacked out. Then I remember hearing a snoring sound, which when I watched it back, found out it was me making the sound. Then I remember thinking I was missing an Air Canada flight for some reason. Then I rolled over and got to my feet, but I was still in dream mode as he was running at me with a ladder. When I landed, it knocked me back into reality. I looked up and saw a huge maple leaf and went, 'Oh, I'm in the ACC.' And then I just see the ladder landing on me again."

Later in the match, both Superstars managed to simultaneously work their way up the ladder. At the top, they exchanged blows before Cena scooped the champ onto his shoulders for the Attitude Adjustment. From sixteen feet in the air, he sent Edge crashing down through two tables. With Edge motionless on the mat, Cena grabbed the gold and his third WWE Championship.

Unlike most champions, Cena refused to celebrate his win. Instead, he simply walked over to his father, who was seated in the first row, hugged him, and walked away emotionless. He later admitted that the brutality of the match went further than he had hoped. He didn't want to get that extreme, but he realized there was no turning back. So he dumped Edge off the giant ladder, grabbed his title, and went home.

31

ONE YEAR

When John Cena grabbed the WWE Championship from the Air Canada Centre ceiling at *Unforgiven*, little did anybody know he was about to embark on a marathon title reign (380 days), the likes of which hadn't been seen for nearly two decades. You have to go back to Randy Savage's 1988 victory

over Ted DiBiase to find the last champion to succeed for at least one full year. In between the two epic reigns, twenty-five different Superstars, not including Savage and Cena, staked claim to the title, but none were able to reach the elusive one-year mark. The closest was Hulk Hogan, who saw his second reign fall just one day short when he lost to Ultimate Warrior at *WrestleMania VI*.

Despite now holding a lofty spot in the annals of WWE, Cena's reign did not get off to a strong start. In November 2006, at *Cyber Sunday*, he was pinned by *SmackDown*'s World Heavyweight Champion King Booker in a Champion of Champions Match that also featured ECW Champion Big Show. But once 2007 came around, Cena was able to rebound and kick his reign into high gear, starting with two impressive victories over Umaga at *New Year's Revolution* and *Royal Rumble*. By the end of January, he added more gold to his résumé when he formed an unlikely team with Shawn Michaels to defeat Randy Orton and Edge for the World Tag Team Championship.

While the Cena and HBK pairing proved popular with fans, the new champs weren't as thrilled with the partnership. From the beginning, neither man fully trusted the other, and their relationship was strained even more after Michaels won a number-one contender's match. As a result, the tag champs would become opponents at *WrestleMania 23*.

Six days before their scheduled showdown, emotions reached a boiling point when HBK inexplicably flattened his partner with Sweet Chin Music during a tag team match. According to Michaels, the move was proof that his patented superkick was undetectable and could very easily end Cena's reign at *WrestleMania*.

But it didn't. John Cena was able to walk away with the victory after forcing HBK to submit to the STF.

In a way, Michaels ended up being half right. The superkick did manage to end one of Cena's reigns—his World Tag Team Championship reign. On the night after *WrestleMania*, HBK turned on his partner, tossing him out of the ring during a tag team battle royal, thus ending their run with the titles.

As spring turned to summer, John Cena's reign picked up even greater steam. Against all odds, he continued to retain the crown despite finding himself in several unenviable positions. At *Backlash* he turned back three comers—Edge, Randy Orton, and HBK—to maintain his reign. At the next two Pay-Per-Views, he thwarted serious challenges by the towering Great Khali. And at the *Great American Bash*, he manhandled the jacked-up former ECW Champion Bobby Lashley.

After the disposal of Randy Orton at *SummerSlam*, many fans assumed nobody would be able to defeat Cena for the WWE Championship. Those fans were right. It wasn't a WWE Superstar who would eventually unseat Cena. It was a freak injury.

On his three-hundred-and-seventy-ninth day as WWE Champion, Cena suffered a torn right pectoral tendon during a match with Mr. Kennedy. Despite the injury, the champ went on to not only finish the match, but also defeat his opponent. After the contest, however, Orton ran to the ring and sent Cena crashing through the announcers' table with an RKO. The Viper then stood over his fallen foe and counted to ten—a brazen message that Orton believed he would end Cena's reign when they met in a Last Man Standing Match at *No Mercy*.

But Cena never made it to *No Mercy*. Orton's attack, coupled with the injury incurred during the Kennedy match, tore Cena's pec completely off the bone. The severity of the injury required surgery, followed by several months of rehabilitation. On October 2, 2007, Mr. McMahon had no choice but to strip Cena of the WWE Championship, thus ending his amazing reign.

32

ONE WILD NIGHT

Over its nearly fifty years of existence, the WWE Championship has seen its fair share of wild nights. Longtime fans often point to February 5, 1988, when Andre the Giant ended Hulk Hogan's four-year reign, only to immediately hand the gold over to Ted DiBiase. Five years later, on April 4, 1993, the

Hulkster was involved in another shocker when he defeated Yokozuna for the title just minutes after the oversized Superstar won it from Bret Hart. More recently, Mr. McMahon became the first non-fulltime competitor to stake claim to the title when he beat Triple H on September 16, 1999. All of these moments certainly represent the most unpredictable of periods for the WWE Championship; but none, however, were as wild as October 7, 2007—the night the title changed hands three times.

Five days after stripping John Cena of the WWE Championship, Mr. McMahon stood in the middle of the ring at the start of *No Mercy*, prepared to make history.

"By the power vested in me as the creator of all things WWE, allow me, ladies and gentlemen, to present to you the new WWE Champion, Randy Orton!"

The WWE chairman handed Orton the title. As fireworks exploded, the smug Superstar held his new prize high, despite the fact that he had done nothing to earn it.

Three years earlier, Orton became the World Heavyweight Champion

Randy Orton, the new WWE champion.

when he emerged victorious from the main event of *SummerSlam* 2004. The new champ admits to being so awed by the magnitude of the situation that he spent hours in the locker room just staring at the title.

"The next thing I knew, the building was empty and I didn't have a ride," says Orton. "I needed security to drive me back to the hotel."

This time around, the Viper didn't have an opportunity to miss his ride. Just minutes into his reign, Triple H came out and challenged the champ to a title match. A mere ten minutes later, the King of Kings had dethroned Orton. The defeat shocked the third-generation Superstar, who couldn't help but think back to *Unforgiven* 2004, when his World Heavyweight Championship reign was cut short by, again, Triple H.

Like Orton, Triple H had little time to relish in his latest glory. Instead, he was put right back to work against Umaga. Luckily for The Game, he was able to survive Umaga, despite a savage assault on his ribs. But little did the champ know that his evening was far from finished. As a former champion, Orton invoked his right to a rematch to be held later that same evening. Longtime Triple H rival Mr. McMahon not only agreed to grant the Legend Killer his wish, but he also made it a Last Man Standing Match.

Still feeling the effects of his previous two WWE Championship encounters, The Game slowly made his way to the ring, where Orton, who had the benefit of two hours' rest, eagerly awaited his chance at redemption. Despite being severely weakened, a courageous Triple H came out of the gate swinging. But after a while, it became painfully clear that a minor miracle would be needed to gain win number three. Picking up where Umaga left off, Orton focused much of his assault on the champ's injured ribs, before hitting him with an RKO onto a steel chair. Later, he hit the Cerebral Assassin with another brain-rattling RKO, this time on the announcers' table. The Game valiantly tried to reach his feet before the referee reached ten, but the punishment of three title matches was too much for the bloodied warrior to overcome.

No Mercy closed with the same image it had opened with: Randy Orton as WWE Champion. In between, however, was three hours of pure war over the WWE's most coveted prize.

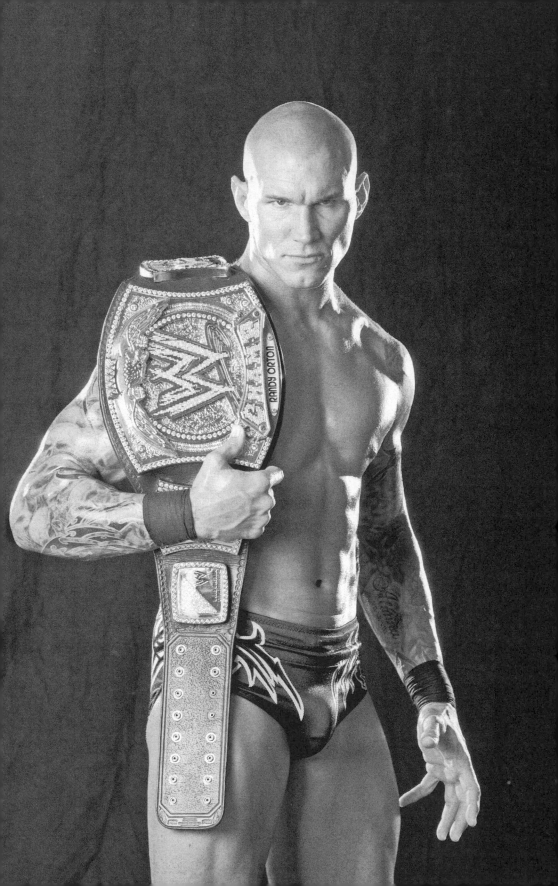

33

THE AGE OF ORTON

You don't have to like Randy Orton, but you do have to appreciate him as a champion. At least that's what Mr. McMahon believed.

One night after the Viper walked away with the gold at *No Mercy*, the WWE chairman planned an elaborate appreciation ceremony in his honor. As part of the event, the boss demanded that every WWE Superstar shake Orton's hand, starting with Triple H. As expected, The Game refused to show up for the ceremony. That's when the champ decided to go to the back and drag his nemesis out himself. Before he could get there, however, Orton was met by a familiar foe from the past—Shawn Michaels.

Five months earlier, the Viper had viciously beat HBK into unconsciousness at *Judgment Day*. The severity of the attack caused Michaels's wife, Rebecca, to dart to her fallen husband's side. She wept uncontrollably, as medical personnel wheeled the future Hall of Famer out of the arena. Many assumed Orton's assault marked the end of Michaels's nearly twenty-five-year career. HBK, however, refused to walk away on a low note. Instead, he tuned up the band, returned to *Raw*, and delivered Sweet Chin Music to the chin of the champ. It wasn't exactly the type of appreciation Orton was expecting.

Upon his return, Michaels was rewarded by the fans with a WWE Championship Match against Orton at *Cyber Sunday*. Unlike most Pay-Per-View events, the interactive element of *Cyber Sunday* allowed viewers to name the matches they want to see. Unfortunately for them, though, they could not dictate the outcome as well. The Legend Killer was able to retain the title after getting disqualified for delivering a low blow to his opponent.

The shady results of *Cyber Sunday* led to another Orton-Michaels match at *Survivor Series*. This time the Viper played by the rules and rode his in-ring prowess to a win, toppling HBK after an RKO.

When Orton helped put John Cena on the shelf back in October, doctors told the Chain Gang Commander he could be out of action for up to one year, which is why his return at the *Royal Rumble* was such a shock. After only four months of inactivity, Cena revealed himself as the surprise thirtieth entry in the Rumble Match. Less than ten minutes later, he punched his ticket to *WrestleMania XXIV* by eliminating Triple H.

Unlike most Rumble winners, Cena claimed he couldn't wait until *WrestleMania* to exact revenge from Orton, so he chose to use his guaranteed title opportunity at *No Way Out* instead. His decision not to compete for the gold at the biggest event of the year was undoubtedly uncommon, but Orton's actions at *No Way Out* certainly were not. For the third time in his reign, Orton got himself disqualified at a Pay-Per-View to retain the title, thus dashing Cena's dreams of regaining the gold. But only temporarily.

Heading into the next night's *Raw*, *WrestleMania*'s WWE Championship Match was already set in stone. It would be Orton defending against Triple H, who won an Elimination Chamber Match at *No Way Out* to earn the honor. This didn't sit well with Cena, who was just twenty-four hours removed from getting screwed out of regaining the title he never lost. After griping about the injustice, the former champ was eventually told he could be added to the *WrestleMania* title match, but only if he could beat Orton in a nontitle match on *Raw*. With The Game serving as special guest referee, Cena capitalized on his golden opportunity, defeating the champ with an Attitude Adjustment. As a result, *WrestleMania XXIV* was changed to a Triple Threat WWE Championship Match, with Orton defending against both Triple H and Cena.

Orton had a laundry list of things working against him at *WrestleMania*. In addition to the rules of a Triple Threat Match heavily favoring the challengers, the third-generation Superstar only had one singles contest on his *WrestleMania* résumé—which he lost to Undertaker at *WrestleMania 21*—while Triple H and Cena had participated in a combined thirteen, winning eight of them. But the Viper refused to let numbers dictate the outcome of his title reign. He was the WWE Champion, and at *WrestleMania* he was going to prove why.

With more than 70,000 rooting against him, Orton delivered a vicious punt to the skull of Triple H. The impact pushed the King of Kings off Cena, who was felled by a Pedigree moments earlier. With both challengers down, the Viper slithered over to Cena and made the cover for the win. Despite the odds being heavily against him, Orton successfully proved he was worthy of being WWE Champion on the grandest stage of them all.

With the title still in his possession, the arrogant champ walked into *Raw* the next night and declared that WWE was now living in the Age of Orton. Little did he know, though, that his days as champion were dwindling.

At *Backlash* in April 2008, Orton was faced with his toughest challenge to date when he defended the gold in an Elimination Match against three former WWE Champions: JBL, Triple H, and Cena. Unlike *Wrestle-*

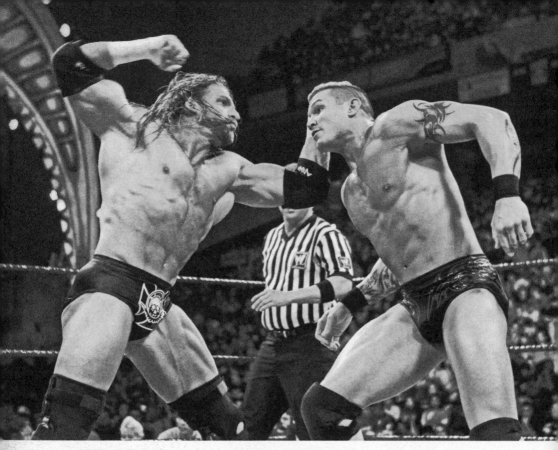

Triple H vs. Randy Orton.

Mania, where the title could've changed hands without Orton being involved in the decision, the Viper controlled his own destiny at *Backlash.* The only thing he had to do was survive three eliminations, a task easier said than done.

Ten minutes into the match, Orton's chances of retaining increased greatly when JBL was eliminated via a Cena STF. Seconds later, the champ helped his own cause by dismissing the Chain Gang Commander following a punt to the head. With just Triple H standing in the way of victory, the self-proclaimed One-Man Dynasty went for his lethal punt, but The Game was able to dodge the champ's foot and hook Orton's arms for the Pedigree. A mere three seconds later, the Age of Orton had ended and Triple H was celebrating his seventh WWE Championship, a then-record shared with The Rock.

34

THE FUTURE IS NOW

When Triple H started Evolution, he personally invited Randy Orton entry into the elite faction, claiming the third-generation Superstar was the future of sports-entertainment. He just didn't expect the future to be 2008, nor did he plan on allowing it to roll through him. To prove he was still the

King of Kings, The Game used the next two Pay-Per-View events to not only beat Orton but maim him as well.

After defeating the Viper in a Steel Cage Match at May's *Judgment Day*, Triple H was ordered by *Raw* General Manager William Regal to defend the gold against Orton yet again. This time they would compete in a contest both Superstars were very familiar with—a Last Man Standing Match.

The previous year, Orton had defeated Triple H to claim the WWE Championship in a match contested under the same rules. Since that time, the Viper had gone on to cement himself as one of the game's greatest Superstars, complete with a near seven-month reign atop *Raw*. Fast forward to June 2008, and Orton was a former champion looking to regain the gold. Current champion Triple H, however, was not ready to relinquish it.

Utilizing the entire arena as their personal playground, the two Superstars victimized each other with a wide array of weaponry. The announcers' table, steel ring steps, cable wire—all were employed. But in the end, it was simply a mistimed RKO that proved to be Orton's undoing.

"I went for the move but got caught, and my momentum actually took me over the top rope," recalls Orton. "On my way down, my foot caught the top rope. I wasn't really in control of my body and I came crashing down on my side. My clavicle just burst; I could feel it break. From that point on, there wasn't really much I could do. He ended it right there."

Not only did Triple H end it, but he added a brutal exclamation point when he nailed Orton with his trusty sledgehammer. From there, the ten count was academic.

Shortly after Triple H disposed of Orton, the WWE Championship was given a new home when The Game was drafted from *Raw* to *SmackDown*. The unexpected move to Friday nights failed to deter the champ; he spent the next several months successfully turning back John Cena, Edge, the Great Khali, and other top names. By September, The Game had proven his worth over nearly every main eventer *SmackDown* had to offer. That's when General Manager Vickie Guerrero offered the opportunity of a lifetime to four Superstars itching to climb up the ladder. At *Unforgiven*, The Brian Kendrick, MVP, Shelton Benjamin, and Jeff Hardy all vied for Triple H's title in the first-ever WWE Championship Scramble Match, a unique twenty-minute contest that crowns interim championship reigns to Superstars who pick up victories during the allotted time. Only the Superstar who registers the final fall is considered the true WWE Champion.

Minus a brief interim championship reign from Kendrick, the majority of the Scramble was dominated by Triple H and Hardy. In the end, The Game walked away with the win, but Hardy's three interim title reigns helped catapult him to main event status, a role that had eluded him for ten years.

The Extreme Enigma's first few months atop the card were a bit shaky, as he fell to The Game at both *No Mercy* and *Cyber Sunday*. But after defeating Triple H in a nontitle match in November, many believed his time to shine was finally coming.

Hardy's road to the WWE Championship took an ugly turn on the morning of *Survivor Series*. At three o'clock that morning—when he should've been in bed resting for the biggest match of his career—Hardy was found unconscious in the stairwell of his Boston hotel. The mainstream media jumped all over the story, assuming the Superstar had suffered a relapse in his battle with drugs. Those outlets eventually had egg on their faces when it was later learned that Jeff was instead attacked by his jealous brother, Matt.

The assault put Hardy's involvement in the *Survivor Series* WWE Championship Triple Threat Match in serious jeopardy. And by match time, there was no sign of the Extreme Enigma, leaving WWE no choice but to convert the match into a one-on-one contest between Triple H and Vladimir Kozlov.

After a little more than ten minutes of action, The Game appeared to have the match won when he connected with his patented Pedigree. But before he could cover his opponent, Vickie Guerrero came to the stage to announce that the match would indeed be a Triple Threat after all.

"Ladies and gentlemen, he's here; he's here!" she said excitedly.

Guerrero pointed to the entryway as the sold-out TD Banknorth Garden rose to their feet expecting to see Hardy. Instead, they got the General Manager's husband, Edge, who had not been seen in WWE since *SummerSlam*, when Undertaker sent him through a fiery hole in the ring mat.

In keeping with his Ultimate Opportunist persona, Edge preyed on his already worn opposition, and within moments of entering the fray, he covered Triple H for the win and his third WWE Championship.

35

HOT POTATO

When Bruno Sammartino won his first WWE Championship in 1963, the wrestling scene was far different than it is today. For the Italian strongman, keeping the title meant turning back the likes of Gene Kiniski, Killer Kowalski, and Giant Baba. While all were greats of their time, they hardly possessed the

Jeff Hardy, king of the mountain at *Armageddon 2008*.

athleticism of today's WWE Superstars. It wasn't until the late 1970s that wrestling rings slowly began to be taken over by larger, more muscular Superstars. As the 1970s made way for the '80s and beyond, sports-entertainment continued to evolve. Those who grew up idolizing "Superstar" Billy Graham and Bob Backlund started to combine their heroes' greatest attributes to create today's Superstar—the ultimate combination of physical conditioning, charisma, and athleticism.

With upwards of one hundred of these "Ultimate Superstars" on the roster at one time, holding the WWE Championship for an extended period of time is considerably harder than it was in Sammartino's day, as evidenced by Edge's victory at *Survivor Series*, which started a game of hot potato that is still being played today.

A mere three weeks after capturing his third WWE Championship, the Rated-R Superstar defended his title against Jeff Hardy and Triple H in the final-ever *Armageddon* Pay-Per-View match. Ironically, both Edge and Hardy were also involved in the event's first-ever match in 1999. In between that time, the two Superstars' careers practically paralleled each other. Together, they grew from "curtain jerkers" into bona fide cult icons, thanks in large part to their daredevil *Tables, Ladders, and Chairs* performances over the World Tag Team Championship. But on this night, the prize was the WWE Championship.

For a moment, it looked like Triple H was on the verge of victory after he Pedigreed champion Edge. But as The Game went for the cover, Hardy delivered his signature Swanton Bomb, which sent Triple H rolling out of the ring. With The Game on the outside, Hardy rolled on top of Edge and made the match-ending cover.

Like Edge before him, Hardy's childhood was spent fantasizing about one day becoming WWE Champion. At *Armageddon*, his dream finally came true, but it wasn't without its fair share of setbacks. In recent years, the Extreme Enigma suffered from a drug dependency, which set him back both personally and professionally. His erratic behavior eventually reached a boiling point in 2003, resulting in WWE severing ties with him completely. After hitting rock bottom, Hardy finally fought to put the pieces of his life back together. He eventually proved himself to WWE and earned his job back in 2006. Fast forward to December 14, 2008, and he was on top of the wrestling world . . . temporarily.

With his brother, Matt, in his corner, Jeff made his first Pay-Per-View title defense against Edge at the 2009 *Royal Rumble*. Heading into the event, Jeff didn't realize that it was Matt who had attacked him from behind on the morning of *Survivor Series*. By the end of the night, however, the truth came out in the most painful of fashions.

Toward the end of the match, Jeff placed a steel chair under the head of his fallen opponent. He then urged his brother to take a second chair and nail the challenger in the head, a move Edge made popular years earlier. Matt jerked the chair back, giving the illusion that he was going to whack the Rated-R Superstar. But instead he floored his own unsuspecting brother. Motionless, Jeff lay on his back while Edge made the cover.

From a personal standpoint, Matt's betrayal drove a huge wedge in the relationship of the two brothers. Professionally, however, it gave Edge his fourth WWE Championship, and one that he would once again have a tough time retaining. Just twenty-one days into his reign, the Rated-R Superstar coughed up the gold in an Elimination Chamber Match at *No Way Out*.

Just minutes into the contest, Edge was surprisingly knocked out of the match when Jeff Hardy rolled him up for the pin. For the next half hour, the WWE Championship had no owner, as five of WWE's top names—Hardy, Triple H, Undertaker, Vladimir Kozlov, and Big Show—battled for the right to take the gold home. In the end, it was Triple H Pedigreeing Undertaker en route to his record eighth WWE Championship reign.

Intermittent Explosive Disorder (IED) is an extremely rare behavioral disorder characterized by impulsive acts of aggression. Oftentimes, the condition manifests itself in uncontrollable fits of rage.

One week after punting the sixty-three-year-old Mr. McMahon into a hospital bed, Randy Orton—surrounded by a team of lawyers and therapists—claimed he was not responsible for his actions against the WWE chairman. Instead, he alleged the attack was caused by his supposed affliction with IED. Orton did little to actually prove he was suffering from the disorder, but the charade was successful in saving the third-generation Superstar from certain termination.

With a new lease on life, it would have been logical for Orton to shift his anger away from sports-entertainment's most powerful family. But

the Legend Killer was never one to take the conventional route. Instead of backing away, he went at the McMahons with even more vigor, complete with a punt to Shane's head and an RKO to Stephanie.

The sight of his children's mother victimized at the hands of the Viper was unbearable for Triple H, who challenged Orton and his Legacy cohorts, Cody Rhodes and Ted DiBiase, to a Handicap Match on *Raw*. During the contest, Orton and DiBiase handcuffed Triple H to the top ring rope. The Legend Killer then grabbed a sledgehammer and threatened to bash the champ's skull. Fearing for her husband's life, Stephanie ran to the ring hoping to stop the slaughter. Instead, she was hit with another RKO.

There was very little The Game could do to save Stephanie. Still cuffed to the rope, he was forced to watch while his rival slithered over his wife's fallen body. Then, with Triple H helplessly watching, Orton slowly kissed Stephanie's lips.

"It was a very powerful situation for me," admits Orton. "I had nothing but time to do what I needed to do that night. After I sealed it with a kiss, I felt like I couldn't get much more heat."

Triple H was able to cool off Orton at *WrestleMania XXV*, but their white-hot personal war was far from being extinguished. At *Backlash*, The Game, Shane McMahon, and Batista squared off against Orton, DiBiase, and Rhodes in a six-man tag team match with a unique twist: If Orton's team won, regardless of which Superstars were involved in the deciding fall, the Legend Killer would be awarded the WWE Championship.

Traditionalists cringed at the thought of one Superstar winning or losing the prestigious WWE title for another. Flashbacks of the dark day Andre the Giant handed the title to DiBiase's father, the Million Dollar Man, occupied their thoughts. Unlike with that historic event, though, winning the gold for somebody else was legal at *Backlash*, meaning there was a very real chance Orton would walk away with the title without being involved in the decision.

By night's end, all concerns were quieted when both Triple H and Orton played a major role in the match's outcome. As The Game attempted to convince Batista not to use a steel chair, the Viper snuck in and dropped the distracted champ with an RKO. Orton went for the pin, but Triple H miraculously kicked out. The sold-out Dunkin' Donuts Center in Providence, Rhode Island, jumped to their feet, anticipating a comeback by the eight-time WWE Champion. But their joy was quickly squashed when Orton went to his patented punt to finally dethrone the King of Kings.

Orton's third WWE title reign closely mimicked his second, as he utilized disqualifications to avoid losing the gold. Sensing a loss to Batista at May's *Judgment Day* nearing, the champ intentionally slapped the referee, resulting in a blatant DQ. The shrewd move saved Orton's reign but did little to rid himself of Batista, a Superstar with whom he owns an extensive history.

"Dave was the first guy I met in OVW in 2000 when I first started," remembers Orton. "We were hand-picked because we both had a lot of potential. There were a lot of positive things we brought to the table. He was the heater, the body. I was an up-and-coming third-generation guy. Even back then, I knew we would have many matches."

Orton was right, and their next would be at the *Extreme Rules* Pay-Per-View in June 2009. This time, though, Orton wouldn't be able to save his title via disqualification. Instead, they would battle in a steel cage, where there are only three ways to win: Escape the steel structure, pinfall, or submission.

Batista.

Heading into the match, Batista had already proven himself a future Hall of Famer. His résumé at the time boasted one WWE Tag Team Championship reign, three World Tag Team Title reigns, and four runs with the prestigious World Heavyweight Championship. But there was always one title that eluded him throughout his highly decorated career—the WWE Championship.

High drama unfolded early in the match, as Orton nearly escaped the structure within seconds of the opening bell. But Batista quickly pulled him off the top of the cage and introduced the champ facefirst into all four sides of the unforgiving steel. Orton never fully recovered from his poor start. After just seven short minutes, the Animal flattened his former Evolution ally with a Batista Bomb to pick up his first-ever WWE title.

The contest proved to be one of the shortest WWE Championship Steel Cage Matches in history. Unfortunately for Batista, his reign also lacked length. The new champ was brutally attacked by Orton, DiBiase, and Rhodes just twenty-four hours after his big win, resulting in a completely torn left biceps for the Animal. Facing surgery and a four-month rehabilitation process, Batista had no choice but to relinquish his newly won title.

For the Animal, the injury marked the second time he was forced to forfeit a world title (in January 2006, he also relinquished the World Heavyweight Championship due to injury). But for Orton, it was an opportunity. On the June 15, 2009, episode of *Raw*, the third-generation Superstar outlasted Triple H, Big Show, and John Cena in a Fatal Four Way Match to reclaim the gold he had lost just one week prior.

36

RANDY ORTON
VERSUS JOHN CENA

Randy Orton's victory on *Raw* marked the fifth WWE Championship exchange over 2009's initial six months, the most the first half of a calendar year had seen since 1999, when the title changed hands an unprecedented seven times over the same period of time. But with the gold back in

Orton's possession, the game of hot potato cooled a bit. For three months, anyway.

After defeating Triple H in a grueling Three Stages of Hell Match at the *Bash*, Orton believed he was finally finished with his former mentor and longtime rival. But *Raw*'s first-ever guest host, Batista, had other plans. With the power to book any matches for the upcoming *Night of Champions* Pay-Per-View, the Animal announced a two-week, single-elimination tournament to crown the number-one contender for Orton's WWE Championship.

With an opportunity to face Orton at *Night of Champions* on the line, Triple H and Cena squared off in the tournament finals. The match marked only the third time these two greats battled in one-on-one competition, with both Superstars picking up a win over the course of their previous two encounters. On this night, however, there would be no decisive victor. Much to the chagrin of the fans, the epic showdown was marred by controversy when Cody Rhodes and Ted DiBiase attacked both men.

The match ended in a double disqualification, leaving Orton to claim that because there was no winner, he wouldn't have to wrestle either man. Unfortunately for Orton, his claims fell on deaf ears. It was later announced that because there was no *loser*, both men would go on to compete against the Viper in a rematch of their classic *WrestleMania XXIV* Triple Threat encounter.

At *Night of Champions*, Orton's reign appeared to come to a premature end when he tapped out. Traditionally, when a Superstar taps out, it signifies the conclusion of the match and, in Orton's case, the end of his WWE Championship reign. But this instance was not so straightforward. The Viper wasn't just giving in to the pressures of one submission hold, but two. Triple H had the champ locked in a Sharpshooter, while Cena cinched in his STF. Fearing permanent injury, Orton tapped wildly.

Confused, the referee didn't know how to proceed. Should he stop the match and award the title to Triple H? Or did it belong to Cena? Before a final decision could be rendered, Rhodes and DiBiase hit the ring and attacked Orton's two challengers, allowing the champ to recover and nail Cena with an RKO to end the match. Just like at *WrestleMania XXIV*, the arrogant Orton proved his worth over two of WWE's greatest, albeit with some help from Legacy.

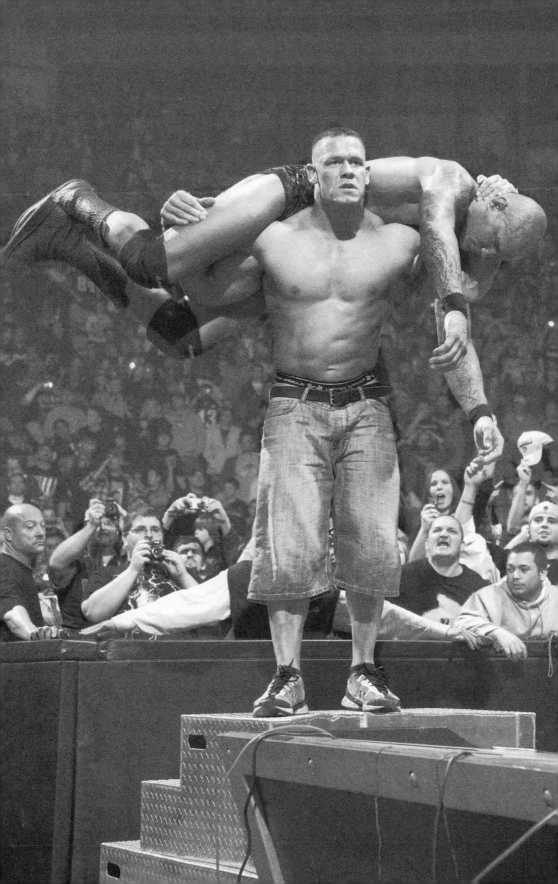

Orton used his typical dastardly tactics to turn back Cena again at *SummerSlam*. This time it was the interference of a supposed fan that carried the Viper to victory. The true identity of the mysterious man was later revealed to be DiBiase's brother, Brett. Regardless of how it happened, though, it was another win for Orton, and he was going to brag about it.

Tired of hearing his champion crow over cheap victories, Mr. McMahon put Orton in a situation that only his skills could get him out of: an "I Quit" Match against Cena at *Breaking Point*. Furthermore, if anybody were to interfere on the champ's behalf, the match would end and Orton would be stripped of his gold.

The last time Orton was backed into such a corner was the *Extreme Rules* Steel Cage Match against Batista. And just like that night, there was nowhere for the Viper to slither off to when he faced Cena. Utilizing his STF submission hold, the Chain Gang Commander forced Orton to utter the words no Superstar ever dreams of saying: "I quit!"

The end of Orton's fourth reign coincidentally also marked the beginning of Cena's. It additionally kicked off yet another series of lightning-quick reigns that carried well into 2010.

Less than one month after once again becoming WWE Champion, Cena returned the title to Orton after falling to the Viper in a Hell in a Cell Match. For Cena, the loss marked the end of his shortest title reign to

John Cena forces Randy Orton to say "I quit!"

that point. Looking back today, though, he is able to put his brief reign in perspective.

"I don't really get bent out of shape over losses. With so many matches—we have *Raw* fifty-two weeks a year and fourteen Pay-Per-Views—nobody can run the table. You're going to lose eventually. You have to be prepared for being able to lose, and you have to be prepared for what you have to do after that. I've never been upset after any loss. I just worry about how I can bounce back."

Cena didn't have to worry about bouncing back for very long. Less than twenty-four hours later, the former champ approached Orton with an idea. According to Cena, their ongoing war wasn't just a rivalry, it was *the* rivalry. And because it was so great, they owed it to the fans to deliver one final sendoff. Over the course of their rivalry, the Superstars were dead-locked at 5–5 against each other in Pay-Per-View battles. This match, said Cena, would finally give the fans one decisive winner. But he didn't want to compete in just any match. He knew they had to battle in *the* match. The ultimate test of endurance. A sixty-minute WWE Iron Man Match.

Realizing his rival was right, Orton accepted, but only if Cena agreed to leave *Raw* if he lost. Cena acquiesced to the stipulation, making it official: At *Bragging Rights*, it would be Randy Orton versus John Cena one final time.

With the fight of his life looming, Orton began an intense training regime that directly contradicted Bret Hart's *WrestleMania XII* WWE Iron Man Match preparations, which featured increased cardio.

"It's hard to train for such a match; you can't really do the elliptical and expect it to get you in ring shape," claims Orton. "So I did a lot of rope drills—hitting the ropes, running the ropes . . . anything I could to get my body toughened up to last an hour in the ring."

Orton and Cena's previous three Pay-Per-View matches lasted sixty minutes *combined*. Armed with this knowledge, many expected the two Superstars to come out slow, pacing themselves for the long and grueling night. But that was not the case. In fact, the first fall came less than four minutes into the match, when Orton tapped to a Cena STF. Just a few minutes later, the champ felled his challenger with an RKO. The match was less than ten minutes old and already both men had recorded a fall.

The remainder of the match continued at a back-and-forth pace. Orton took a 5–4 lead into the final ten minutes, but Cena was able to tie the score after delivering a back-breaking Attitude Adjustment through the announcers' table. With possible overtime looming, the Viper looked to take the lead with one minute left on the clock. He reared back for his trademark punt, but Cena wisely sidestepped the debilitating kick and countered into the STF. Refusing to let their epic rivalry go in Cena's favor, Orton with-stood the punishment for more than fifty seconds. But finally, with only four seconds left on the clock, the pain became too great. Orton tapped, ending his fifth WWE Championship reign and one of the most intense ri-valries ever seen.

37

A NEW THREAT

When Jesse Ventura agreed to guest host *Raw* in November 2009, WWE knew the opinionated former Superstar would shake things up. They just didn't realize how much.

Tired of seeing the likes of Randy Orton, Triple H, and Shawn Michaels constantly featured in championship matches, Ventura introduced a revolutionary concept he called the Break-through Battle Royal. The winner would be awarded a championship opportunity against John Cena at *WWE TLC: Tables, Ladders, and Chairs.* The only prerequisite to qualify for the match was that the Superstar must never have previously held a world title.

The Battle Royal featured WWE's brightest upstarts: Kofi Kingston, Cody Rhodes, Ted DiBiase, MVP, R-Truth, Mark Henry, and Sheamus. It also included former WWE Champion Randy Orton, who weaseled his way around Ventura's stipulation.

Orton appeared to be the match's odds-on favorite, considering his past championship experience. As a result, many fans watched with a skeptical eye, assuming they would not get the new-look challenger Ventura promised. But when the Viper was eliminated late in the contest, the Giant Center in Hershey, Pennsylvania, perked up. They were finally going to see the fresh face they wanted. In the end, it was Sheamus knocking Kingston over the top to earn the right to face Cena in a Tables Match at *WWE TLC.*

Prior to the event, the Celtic Warrior put the entire WWE on notice—both Superstars and employees—with his never-before-seen level of aggression. He brutally assaulted a timekeeper, inexplicably attacked announcer Jerry Lawler, and even beat Jamie Noble into retirement. But despite his impressive wake of destruction, few gave Sheamus a chance on the big stage against Cena.

Perhaps even the champ underestimated the Celtic Warrior. Assuming he had Sheamus in a vulnerable state atop the turnbuckle, Cena climbed the ring ropes, looking to execute a Superplex. But Sheamus's power proved superior, as he sent Cena sailing through a table situated on the mat. With that, Cena's fifth stay at the top came to an end, while Sheamus's surprising WWE Championship reign was just beginning.

"It was one of the most surreal moments of my life," recalls Sheamus. "If you watch me closely, I kept looking at the gold to make sure it was real and was actually in my hand. The rest is a blur."

Sheamus's victory at *WWE TLC* capped off the second quickest rise to the WWE Championship in history (only Brock Lesnar got there faster). After only five and a half months, the fiery-haired Superstar had reached a level many on the roster have been fighting years to achieve. William Regal. Matt Hardy. Christian: Combined, these amazing Superstars have

Sheamus victorious over John Cena.

logged nearly sixty years of professional service. Yet none of them have been able to accomplish what the Celtic Warrior did in less than six months.

"Of course I sense a certain level of animosity or jealousy," says Sheamus. "And I love it! I was the WWE Champion, and anyone who strives to be the best wants to be in my position. If the shoe was on the other foot, I would be jealous too. But it's not, and I'm enjoying every minute of it."

For the next seventy days, the first-ever Irish-born WWE Champion continued on his impressive path of destruction. He plowed through MVP, Evan Bourne, and Christian en route to what appeared to be a spot in the main event at the biggest show of the year. But before Sheamus could consider himself a *WrestleMania* headliner, he needed to survive sixteen tons of the Elimination Chamber's unforgiving steel.

Two miles of chainlink surrounded the champ and his five rabid challengers—Triple H, Cena, Kingston, Orton, and DiBiase—as the bell rang, signifying the final leg on the road to *WrestleMania*. Unfortunately for Sheamus, it also marked the closing moments of his impressive WWE Championship reign. After nearly thirty minutes of dodging bullets, the Celtic Warrior was finally taken down by a Pedigree at the hands of Triple H.

Sheamus's elimination guaranteed the crowning of a new champion. Only Triple H and Cena remained, but both men were feeling the effects of the career-altering contest. Unable to get to his feet, Cena slowly rolled over to The Game and cinched in his signature STF. Triple H clawed for the safety of the bottom rope, but Cena's grip was too powerful to overcome. Slowly losing consciousness, the Cerebral Assassin was left with no other choice but to tap out.

Cena's victory assured him a spot in *WrestleMania*'s main event. Or so he thought. Seconds after surviving the punishing Elimination Chamber, the new WWE Champion was forced to overcome yet another lofty obstacle when Mr. McMahon announced that his enforcer, Batista, would be challenging for the title right then and there.

The situation was eerily reminiscent of the 2006 *New Year's Revolution* Elimination Chamber, where Cena amazingly survived thirty minutes of grueling action only to have his gold plucked away by Edge minutes after the match. Hoping history would not repeat itself, the exhausted champ made the first move, hitting Batista with a right hand. The weakened punch, however, angered the Animal more than anything else. Batista then charged at the champ and connected with a rib-rattling spear. The match could have very easily ended there, but instead the challenger added insult to injury, flattening the Chain Gang Commander with a Batista Bomb before finally putting him out of his misery. Less than one minute into his sixth WWE Championship reign, Cena had already lost the gold.

Prior to Batista's thievery of Cena's title, the two Superstars shared very little history. The brief past they did have, however, all leaned in the Animal's favor. In January 2005, he last eliminated the Chain Gang Commander to win the *Royal Rumble*. And three years after that, he pinned Cena's shoulders to the mat at *SummerSlam* 2008. Though the sample size was small, it was enough to make Batista the heavy favorite heading into their *Wrestle-Mania XXVI* showdown.

History looked to repeat itself after the Animal delivered a thunderous Batista Bomb to the challenger. But Cena miraculously kicked out behind the support of more than 72,000 screaming fans at the sold-out University of Phoenix Stadium in Glendale, Arizona. Back on the offensive, the challenger slapped on his STF and continued to apply pressure until Batista was forced to tap out.

The win gave Cena his seventh WWE Championship, tying him with The Rock for the second most reigns in WWE history. Only Triple H has more.

38

THE NEXT WWE CHAMPION

The WWE Championship's first five decades saw the image of

the ideal titleholder go through several transformations. In its

earliest days, the gold was anchored by the quiet fan favorites

with strong ethnic ties, such as Bruno Sammartino and Pedro

Morales. As time passed, pure technical ability took a backseat to body mass and charisma, as evidenced by Hulk Hogan and Ultimate Warrior. In the late 1990s, Stone Cold Steve Austin brought a new rebellious attitude to the title. And today's champions, such as Triple H and John Cena, possess a never-say-die mindset that has carried them through the most brutal battles the WWE title has ever seen.

Considering the wide range of Superstars who have held the WWE Championship in the past, it's impossible to pinpoint who tomorrow's titlists will be. Names like The Miz, Kofi Kingston, Ted DiBiase, and Drew McIntyre appear to be the next set of young men tasked with taking the title into 2010 and beyond. For them, the WWE Championship represents an opportunity to permanently etch their names into the record books, while also earning entry into WWE's most elite fraternity, alongside Bret Hart, Shawn Michaels, and The Rock, among others.

But as every past champion can attest, success is fleeting. Despite their best efforts to stay atop the roster, time eventually catches up to them. And while it's hard to imagine now, the Kingstons and McIntyres of the world will also be forced to hang up their boots someday. When this happens, who will step up to fill their shoes?

When looking over the list of past WWE Champions, the one constant these Superstars share is their lifelong fandom of sports-entertainment. Before they ever set foot inside a ring, names like Cena and Edge were young boys who dreamed of one day wrapping the gold around their waist. And if history is any indication of who tomorrow's WWE Champion will be, there's a very good chance it will be a lifelong fan. It could be that young man in the Randy Orton T-shirt you see seated ringside at *Raw*. Or the one who makes sure he's first in line on the morning *WrestleMania* tickets go on sale. It could even be somebody reading this very book. It might very well be you!

WWE CHAMPIONSHIP TIMELINE

APRIL 29, 1963, RIO DE JANEIRO

Buddy Rogers defeats Antonino Rocca

Note: Buddy Rogers beat Antonino Rocca in the finals of a tournament to be crowned the first-ever WWE Champion.

MAY 17, 1963, NEW YORK, NY

Bruno Sammartino defeats Buddy Rogers

JANUARY 18, 1971, NEW YORK, NY

Ivan Koloff defeats Bruno Sammartino

FEBRUARY 8, 1971, NEW YORK, NY

Pedro Morales defeats Ivan Koloff

DECEMBER 1, 1973, PHILADELPHIA, PA

Stan Stasiak defeats Pedro Morales

DECEMBER 10, 1973, NEW YORK, NY

Bruno Sammartino defeats Stan Stasiak

APRIL 30, 1977, BALTIMORE, MD
"Superstar" Billy Graham defeats Bruno Sammartino

FEBRUARY 20, 1978, NEW YORK, NY
Bob Backlund defeats "Superstar" Billy Graham

DECEMBER 26, 1983, NEW YORK, NY
The Iron Sheik defeats Bob Backlund

JANUARY 23, 1984, NEW YORK, NY
Hulk Hogan defeats the Iron Sheik

FEBRUARY 5, 1988, INDIANAPOLIS, IN
Andre the Giant defeats Hulk Hogan
Note: WWE President Jack Tunney vacated the title after learning that Ted DiBiase had paid a corrupt referee to have plastic surgery in order to look like the official referee assigned to the match.

MARCH 27, 1988, ATLANTIC CITY, NJ
Randy Savage defeats Ted DiBiase
Note: Randy Savage beat Ted DiBiase in the finals of a fourteen-man, one-night tournament to crown a new WWE Champion.

APRIL 2, 1989, ATLANTIC CITY, NJ
Hulk Hogan defeats Randy Savage

APRIL 1, 1990, TORONTO, ONTARIO
Ultimate Warrior defeats Hulk Hogan

JANUARY 19, 1991, MIAMI, FL
Sgt. Slaughter defeats Ultimate Warrior

MARCH 24, 1991, LOS ANGELES, CA
Hulk Hogan defeats Sgt. Slaughter

NOVEMBER 27, 1991, DETROIT, MI
Undertaker defeats Hulk Hogan

DECEMBER 3, 1991, SAN ANTONIO, TX

Hulk Hogan defeats Undertaker

Note: WWE President Jack Tunney vacated the title due to controversy surrounding Hulk Hogan's win over Undertaker.

JANUARY 19, 1992, ALBANY, NY

Ric Flair wins WWE Championship

Note: Ric Flair won the WWE Championship after last eliminating Sid Justice from the *Royal Rumble*.

APRIL 5, 1992, INDIANAPOLIS, IN

Randy Savage defeats Ric Flair

SEPTEMBER 1, 1992, HERSHEY, PA

Ric Flair defeats Randy Savage

OCTOBER 12, 1992, SASKATOON, SASKATCHEWAN

Bret Hart defeats Ric Flair

APRIL 4, 1993, LAS VEGAS, NV

Yokozuna defeats Bret Hart

APRIL 4, 1993, LAS VEGAS, NV

Hulk Hogan defeats Yokozuna

JUNE 13, 1993 DAYTON, OH

Yokozuna defeats Hulk Hogan

MARCH 20, 1994, NEW YORK, NY

Bret Hart defeats Yokozuna

NOVEMBER 23, 1994, SAN ANTONIO, TX

Bob Backlund defeats Bret Hart

NOVEMBER 26, 1994, NEW YORK, NY

Diesel defeats Bob Backlund

NOVEMBER 19, 1995, LANDOVER, MD
Bret Hart defeats Diesel

MARCH 31, 1996, ANAHEIM, CA
Shawn Michaels defeats Bret Hart

NOVEMBER 17, 1996, NEW YORK, NY
Sid defeats Shawn Michaels

JANUARY 19, 1997, SAN ANTONIO, TX
Shawn Michaels defeats Sid

FEBRUARY 16, 1997, CHATTANOOGA, TN
Bret Hart defeats Undertaker
Note: After injuries forced Shawn Michaels to vacate the title, Bret Hart last eliminated Undertaker in a Fatal Four Way Match that also included Stone Cold Steve Austin and Vader.

FEBRUARY 17, 1997, NASHVILLE, TN
Sid defeats Bret Hart

MARCH 23, 1997, CHICAGO, IL
Undertaker defeats Sid

AUGUST 3, 1997, EAST RUTHERFORD, NJ
Bret Hart defeats Undertaker

NOVEMBER 9, 1997, MONTREAL, QUEBEC
Shawn Michaels defeats Bret Hart

MARCH 29, 1998, BOSTON, MA
Stone Cold Steve Austin defeats Shawn Michaels

JUNE 28, 1998, PITTSBURGH, PA
Kane defeats Stone Cold Steve Austin

JUNE 29, 1998, CLEVELAND, OH

Stone Cold Steve Austin defeats Kane

Note: Mr. McMahon vacated the title in September 1998 following a controversial ending to a Triple Threat Match featuring Undertaker vs. Kane vs. Stone Cold Steve Austin.

NOVEMBER 15, 1998, ST. LOUIS, MO

The Rock defeats Mankind

Note: The Rock last defeated Mankind in a fourteen-man, one-night tournament to crown a new WWE Champion.

JANUARY 4, 1999, WORCESTER, MA

Mankind defeats The Rock

JANUARY 24, 1999, ANAHEIM, CA

The Rock defeats Mankind

JANUARY 31, 1999, TUCSON, AZ

Mankind defeats The Rock

FEBRUARY 15, 1999, BIRMINGHAM, AL

The Rock defeats Mankind

MARCH 28, 1999, PHILADELPHIA, PA

Stone Cold Steve Austin defeats The Rock

MAY 23, 1999, KANSAS CITY, MO

Undertaker defeats Stone Cold Steve Austin

JUNE 28, 1999, CHARLOTTE, NC

Stone Cold Steve Austin defeats Undertaker

AUGUST 22, 1999, MINNEAPOLIS, MN

Mankind defeats Stone Cold Steve Austin

Note: Mankind pinned Stone Cold Steve Austin to win the WWE Championship in a Triple Threat Match that also included Triple H.

AUGUST 23, 1999, AMES, IA
Triple H defeats Mankind

SEPTEMBER 16, 1999, LAS VEGAS, NV
Mr. McMahon defeats Triple H
Note: Mr. McMahon vacated the title on September 20, 1999.

SEPTEMBER 26, 1999, CHARLOTTE, NC
Triple H defeats The Rock
Note: Triple H pinned The Rock to win the WWE Championship in a Six-Pack Challenge Match that also included Big Show, Mankind, the British Bulldog, and Kane.

NOVEMBER 14, 1999, DETROIT, MI
Big Show defeats Triple H
Note: Big Show pinned Triple H to win the WWE Championship in a Triple Threat Match that also included The Rock.

JANUARY 3, 2000, MIAMI, FL
Triple H defeats Big Show

APRIL 30, 2000, WASHINGTON, DC
The Rock defeats Triple H

MAY 21, 2000, LOUISVILLE, KY
Triple H defeats The Rock

JUNE 25, 2000, BOSTON, MA
The Rock defeats Mr. McMahon
Note: The Rock, Undertaker, and Kane battled Triple H, Shane, and Mr. McMahon in a six-man Tag Team Match. Prematch stipulations stated that if anybody on The Game's team lost, Triple H would lose the WWE Championship. The Rock pinned Mr. McMahon to win the gold.

OCTOBER 22, 2000, ALBANY, NY
Kurt Angle defeats The Rock

FEBRUARY 25, 2001, LAS VEGAS, NV
The Rock defeats Kurt Angle

APRIL 1, 2001, HOUSTON, TX
Stone Cold Steve Austin defeats The Rock

SEPTEMBER 23, 2001, PITTSBURGH, PA
Kurt Angle defeats Stone Cold Steve Austin

OCTOBER 8, 2001, INDIANAPOLIS, IN
Stone Cold Steve Austin defeats Kurt Angle

DECEMBER 9, 2001, SAN DIEGO, CA
Chris Jericho defeats Stone Cold Steve Austin

MARCH 17, 2002, TORONTO, ONTARIO
Triple H defeats Chris Jericho

APRIL 21, 2002, KANSAS CITY, MO
Hulk Hogan defeats Triple H

MAY 19, 2002, NASHVILLE, TN
Undertaker defeats Hulk Hogan

JULY 21, 2002, DETROIT, MI
The Rock defeats Kurt Angle
Note: The Rock pinned Kurt Angle to win the WWE Championship in a Triple Threat Match that also included then-champ Undertaker.

AUGUST 25, 2002, UNIONDALE, NY
Brock Lesnar defeats The Rock

NOVEMBER 17, 2002, NEW YORK, NY
Big Show defeats Brock Lesnar

DECEMBER 15, 2002, FORT LAUDERDALE, FL
Kurt Angle defeats Big Show

MARCH 30, 2003, SEATTLE, WA
Brock Lesnar defeats Kurt Angle

JULY 27, 2003, DENVER, CO
Kurt Angle defeats Brock Lesnar
Note: Kurt Angle pinned Brock Lesnar to win the WWE Championship in a Triple Threat Match that also included Big Show.

SEPTEMBER 18, 2003, RALEIGH, NC
Brock Lesnar defeats Kurt Angle

FEBRUARY 15, 2004, SAN FRANCISCO, CA
Eddie Guerrero defeats Brock Lesnar

JUNE 27, 2004, NORFOLK, VA
JBL defeats Eddie Guerrero

APRIL 3, 2005, LOS ANGELES, CA
John Cena defeats JBL

JANUARY 8, 2006, ALBANY, NY
Edge defeats John Cena

JANUARY 29, 2006, MIAMI, FL
John Cena defeats Edge

JUNE 11, 2006, NEW YORK, NY
Rob Van Dam defeats John Cena

JULY 3, 2006, PHILADELPHIA, PA
Edge defeats Rob Van Dam
Note: Edge pinned Rob Van Dam to win the WWE Championship in a Triple Threat Match that also included John Cena.

SEPTEMBER 17, 2006, TORONTO, ONTARIO
John Cena defeats Edge

OCTOBER 7, 2007, CHICAGO, IL
Randy Orton is awarded the WWE Championship
Note: Mr. McMahon awarded the WWE Championship to Randy Orton after an injury forced John Cena to surrender the title.

OCTOBER 7, 2007, CHICAGO, IL
Triple H defeats Randy Orton

OCTOBER 7, 2007, CHICAGO, IL
Randy Orton defeats Triple H

APRIL 27, 2008, BALTIMORE, MD
Triple H defeats Randy Orton
Note: Triple H pinned Randy Orton to win the WWE Championship in a Fatal Four Way Match that also included JBL and John Cena.

NOVEMBER 23, 2008, BOSTON, MA
Edge defeats Triple H
Note: Edge pinned Triple H to win the WWE Championship in a Triple Threat Match that also included Vladimir Kozlov.

DECEMBER 14, 2008, BUFFALO, NY
Jeff Hardy defeats Edge
Note: Jeff Hardy pinned Edge to win the WWE Championship in a Triple Threat Match that also included Triple H.

JANUARY 25, 2009, DETROIT, MI
Edge defeats Jeff Hardy

FEBRUARY 15, 2009, SEATTLE, WA
Triple H wins WWE Championship
Note: Triple H won the title after outlasting Edge, Vladimir Kozlov, Jeff Hardy, Undertaker, and Big Show in an Elimination Chamber Match.

APRIL 26, 2009, PROVIDENCE, RI

Randy Orton defeats Triple H

Note: Randy Orton teamed with Cody Rhodes and Ted DiBiase to defeat Triple H, Batista, and Shane McMahon. Prematch stipulations stated that if any member of The Game's team lost, Orton would win the title. In the end, Orton pinned Triple H to gain the gold.

JUNE 7, 2009, NEW ORLEANS, LA

Batista defeats Randy Orton

Note: An injury caused Batista to vacate the title on June 9, 2009.

JUNE 15, 2009, CHARLOTTE, NC

Randy Orton wins WWE Championship

Note: Randy Orton won the title after defeating Triple H, John Cena, and Big Show in a Fatal Four Way Match.

SEPTEMBER 13, 2009, MONTREAL, QUEBEC

John Cena defeats Randy Orton

OCTOBER 4, 2009, NEWARK, NJ

Randy Orton defeats John Cena

OCTOBER 25, 2009, PITTSBURGH, PA

John Cena defeats Randy Orton

DECEMBER 13, 2009, SAN ANTONIO, TX

Sheamus defeats John Cena

FEBRUARY, 21, 2010, ST. LOUIS, MO

John Cena wins WWE Championship

Note: John Cena won the title after outlasting Sheamus, Randy Orton, Triple H, Ted DiBiase Jr., and Kofi Kingston in an Elimination Chamber Match.

FEBRUARY, 21, 2010, ST. LOUIS, MO

Batista defeats John Cena

MARCH 28, 2010, PHOENIX, AZ

John Cena defeats Batista

JUNE 20, 2010, UNIONDALE, NY

Sheamus wins WWE Championship

Note: Sheamus won the title after defeating John Cena, Randy Orton, and Edge in a Fatal Four Way Match.

ACKNOWLEDGMENTS

The WWE Championship didn't become sports-entertainment's

most prestigious prize by accident. Instead, its lofty status is

the result of an unparalleled dedication put forth from the

countless men and women working both in the ring and be-

hind the scenes with WWE over the past five decades. So

to Buddy Rogers, John Cena, the cameramen, the marketing department, everybody at the television studio, Howie in the mailroom, the publications department, and everybody in between—I thank you. I thank you for all your hard work in making the WWE Championship the richest prize in the industry. Without you, this book would never have happened.

Similarly, the book you are holding in your hands right now is as impressive as it is thanks in large part to the amazing team at Simon & Schuster. Thank you to Anthony Ziccardi, Ed Schlesinger, and their entire crew for all of their efforts.

A special thank you to Dean Miller for thinking of me when this project popped up.

I hope you found the quotes in this book to be both entertaining and informative. Sitting down and talking to the past champions was one of the most enjoyable parts of this project, and it couldn't have happened without a select few who searched far and wide to find the former champs. Ann Russo-Gordon, Mark Carrano, and Chris Chambers—thank you for your help.

Thank you to my former WWE colleagues who helped me during the research and writing portion of this book: Katie Raymond-Santo, Frank Vitucci, Howard Finkel, Craig Tello, Jim Ross, Jon Lane, and Mike Archer.

Thank you to Michael Spirito and Nicole Zussman who supported my desire to chronicle the history of the WWE Championship. And thank you to Joe Auriemma and Chris Shearn for allowing me to skip dinner plans for ten straight nights so that I could write.

And last, but certainly not least, thank you to my amazing family, most notably my beautiful wife and son. Oftentimes, my passion for this project left my wife to play the role of both mother *and* father, which she did without even blinking an eye. Thank you both for your patience. I love you!

—Kevin Sullivan, August 2010